Published 2024
Printed in the United States of America
Print ISBN: 978-1-64742-702-3
E-ISBN: 978-1-64742-703-0
Library of Congress Control Number: 2024906628

For information, address:
She Writes Press
1569 Solano Ave #546
Berkeley, CA 94707

Interior Design by Tabitha Lahr

She Writes Press is a division of SparkPoint Studio, LLC.

The WOMAN *in the* ROOM

A Jewish Life
Through 100 Years
of History

NAOMI B. LEVINE
with Sofia Groopman

SHE WRITES PRESS

To Joan Kiddon

If I could turn back the hands of time, I would certainly play it differently. But since I cannot, all I can do is tell you how much I loved you in the past and in the present, and thank you for Chloé, Olivia, and Elowen.

A Special Thank You
to Leonard Stern

When I retired from New York University as its senior vice president for external affairs, I took on several consulting jobs to make up for the income I had lost. As a result, I did not have the time to write this book and others that I had been developing in my mind for many years. Leonard Stern, a remarkable philanthropist, generously included the cause of my writing in his philanthropic efforts, and as a result I was able to give up my consulting jobs and concentrate on writing. The book you hold in your hands is a result of Leonard Stern's philanthropy, which gave me the time and support I needed to write. I want to take this opportunity to thank Leonard Stern very much. I could not have written this book without him.

Contents

Preface

— ★ —

O ver the years, my friends and family have urged me to write
a memoir of my life. I am ninety-seven years old and have
lived, therefore, almost one hundred years—a century. I have
seen immense changes in the world, and, because of the positions
I have held as national executive director of the American
Jewish Congress and then as senior vice president of New York
University, I have met and worked with some extraordinary
people on the world stage. In addition, as a lawyer and as an
activist, I fought for civil rights, human rights, and women's rights
in this country and abroad, so I can honestly say that in some
small measure, I was directly involved in the political, social, and
economic issues that have defined this century.

And yet, I resisted writing a memoir. It seemed vain to believe
that anyone would be interested in reading about my life.

But I am a history buff. I love history. So, I worked out a compromise: this book is half history and half memoir. It explores the
ways in which the history of the past hundred years influenced my
life, while at the same time examining how my life played a role in
that history. As I tell the story of my life and the world around me,
I will move chronologically from the 1920s to 2020. I had initially
planned to stop in the year 2000, but with the election of Donald

J. Trump, who I believe is the one of the worst presidents this country has ever seen, I felt I had to include the present moment.

"What's past is prologue," Shakespeare wrote in *The Tempest*—and so my hope is that my life and the history that shaped me will contain lessons for the future as well.

chapter one

The Child is
the Father of the Man

I am ninety-seven years of age. I can hardly believe it. But I have
in my hand my birth certificate, and so it must be so.

I'm not exactly a good-looking woman. Age has added
hundreds of wrinkles to my face, which have made me even less
attractive (I could begin to use Botox, but I'm told that maybe
it's too late). Still, I have always been able to depend on my brain
(which, thank God, is still working). So, even at this old age, I
have nothing to complain about.

I write this sitting at the window of my NYU apartment at
29 Washington Square West, across the street from Washington
Square Park. Every park has its own personality and voice. Central
Park, for example, speaks of elegance and stability. On its east side,
it is bordered by Fifth Avenue, one of the most beautiful avenues
in the city. On its west side, it is bordered by Central Park West,
also a very beautiful street. Important and affluent people live on

both avenues. They have given generously to Central Park and thus made it the "jewel" of New York City. That park is kept beautiful and elegant. It reflects, in many ways, the faces and the voices of the people who live on either side and support it. But my muse is Washington Square Park, and I must admit it is very different from its more refined uptown cousin. It has a different voice and a different personality—and yet it has such energy. This park is the centerpiece of the campus of NYU, where I spent many, many years working, and it is filled with young people day and night. The students are either marching, complaining, or making love on the walkways and benches and lawns. It is surrounded by NYU's buildings, some in good repair, like the one I live in (which, I must mention Eleanor Roosevelt happened to have lived in from 1942 to 1949; since I was, and still am, a great fan of Eleanor, this makes this apartment very special to me), and some rather shabby. Still, it brings me joy to see the area thriving—for decades it was my mission to ensure that there would always be life on this campus, and therefore in this park. Today, it does feel like I succeeded.

The centerpiece of the park is its beautiful Washington Square Arch, which was built in 1892 to celebrate the centennial of George Washington's 1789 inauguration. Renowned architect Sanford White designed the arch, which he modeled after the Arc de Triomphe in Paris. The arch is a paean to liberty, and the voice of the park that surrounds it is that of youth, struggle, hope, and dreams. If ever there is another revolution in the United States (and I hope that this will never be), you can be sure that the first words that are spoken to inspire the revolution will take place in Washington Square Park, under the arch.

Washington Square Park is beautiful today. Several years ago, it was filled with drug addicts and dealers. Then the university and the New York City Parks Department decided that since the park and NYU's campus are great tourist attractions, they would fix it up. They planted new bushes, elegant flower beds, and more lawns. They repaired the central fountain, so it runs at regular hours, and they cleaned the beautiful marble arch. The park now adds immeasurably to the view from my desk.

One day, not that long ago, I was looking out of the window, as I am now, when a parade of about a hundred people passed me by. The march was in support of Kamala Harris, who was running for president of the United States. At the time, she was one of six women running for this office. Keep in mind that there are already women who are governors of states throughout the country, women members of the Senate and the House of Representatives, women cabinet members, ambassadors, college presidents, I could go on and on, but as I watched the people pass me by, I kept reminding myself that only three years before I was born, this parade could not have happened. Yes, only three years before I was born, women could not vote, sit on juries, bring lawsuits, own property, get custody of their children in the event of a divorce, and they certainly could not run for the presidency of the United States. What brought on this enormous change? At first glance, it seems like a miracle.

But as I thought about it more, I knew this enormous social and political change was no miracle. It was the result of a few women who began the struggle for those rights in the 1800s. They had very little help outside of their small group of suffragettes. They marched, they petitioned government officials, they protested in front of the White House, they were arrested, they held meeting after meeting in various towns throughout the country where they were harassed, jeered at, laughed at, imprisoned, and often denied a space to hold their meetings.

Because of them, today I can not only vote, but own property, bring lawsuits, control my own money, and fight in court for the custody of my child. Because of them, I am a lawyer and have been able to hold two important positions as the national executive director of the American Jewish Congress and as senior vice president of NYU. Even now, I am still an active participant in the politics of my country. I owe this all to a few women who made suffrage the case of their lives. Thank you, Elizabeth Cady Stanton, Susan B. Anthony, Lucretia Mott, and all the other heroines of this struggle. I could not help but think of these extraordinary women as I watched Kamala Harris's many supporters march by my window.

As I looked more carefully, I also saw that some of the people marching were holding signs in different languages. It was heartwarming to realize that this is still a country of immigrants. Many of us are either immigrants ourselves or are the children, grandchildren, or great-grandchildren of immigrants.

I, myself, am the grandchild of an immigrant. I am here today enjoying the fruits of this great country, its freedom, prosperity, and the education it gave me, because my grandfather, an immigrant, faced the terror of crossing the dark and frightening 3,000 miles of the Atlantic Ocean to come to this country.

So, from my perch above the park, I felt that I saw before me two great social transformations of the dawn of the twentieth century that made my life possible. The march for Kamala was witness to the fruits of the suffragist movement and to the opening of the country to immigrants. As I observed the stream of people passing below my window, I felt the march of history, and I thought not only of the suffragettes—great, public heroes—but also of my grandfather, David Mermelstein, a man who is unknown to the history books but whose personal bravery makes him a hero to me.

———

David Mermelstein came to America from Austria at the dawn of the 1900s, a time when there were 13.5 million immigrants living in the United States. He and his fellow immigrants endured the treacherous journey to this country for various reasons. Some were escaping political or religious persecution, some were seeking to avoid the twenty-five-year enlistment in the army that some European countries demanded of Jewish men, and some were simply pursuing opportunity, the promise of a better life. For many, it was some combination of the three.

Jews were particularly eager to come to America, as life for them in Europe was often a very unpleasant and frightening experience. At the time, European Jews were limited in the kinds of business they could conduct. They could not buy property, nor could they work for the government, and they lived in fear of pogroms, which could come at any time and could kill them and their families. In some countries, they were forced to live in communities separated by walls and gates from their Christian neighbors in what were called ghettos. The gates to the ghetto would shut at about 9 p.m. every night, and they had to be within their closed compound by that time or they would be punished.

Whenever my grandfather's mother heard the marching steps of soldiers coming toward their village, she would hide my grandfather in the well on their property. Later in life, whenever he saw a well, his stomach would tighten, haunted by memories of the marching feet of soldiers from long ago. He was a child of the pogroms and the many violent conflicts that were part of his world. He never outgrew the trauma of those years. That's why my grandfather's parents wanted him to come to America. That's why immigration during this period was so high. There was so little opportunity for him and others like him to live a decent life in Europe. My grandfather said that his mother would often say to him, "Oh, my little David, you will go to America and become a successful American man, and then you will come back and take all of us to America."

My grandfather wasn't sure what she meant by "a successful American man," but he always assumed it meant a rich man with lots of money. So, when he was somewhere between fifteen and seventeen years old (we're not sure of the exact year), my great-grandparents saved up enough money to buy my grandfather a one-way ticket in steerage to go to America. Can you imagine putting your child, who might be as young as ten to fifteen years old, on a boat to go 3,000 miles away and perhaps never see him or her again? But conditions for many people, and certainly for Jews, were so bad in Europe at this time that many mothers and fathers did exactly that.

Curious to know more about what steerage travel meant exactly, I turned to a recently published book by the writer Daniel Okrent about immigration. Okrent writes:

> Steerage travel was perfected by Albert Ballin, a lower middle-class Jew from Hamburg who eventually rose to become the chief executive of the Mammoth Hamburg American line. At one point, Ballin had 175 ships at his command—a fleet larger than the merchant marine of any European power, except Germany itself. Hamburg-American vessels had been coming to America to ferry timber and other products eastward to Europe. Contemplating the empty, wasted space on the west-bound trip, Ballin conjured up a commodity that could fill his boats, a commodity far more valuable than timber: immigrants. As it happened, filling a vessel with hundreds of passengers had a subsidiary benefit: the added ballast made the ship easier to steer.[1]

Now, more than a hundred years later, it is extraordinary to imagine my grandfather as "a commodity more valuable than timber." I wondered, though, what it would have been really like to travel in this way. Luckily for me, my friend Joan Dims recently published a terrific book on the Statue of Liberty called *Lady Liberty*. In it she talks about her grandmother, Ida, who, like my grandfather, came over to the United States in steerage. She writes:

> The voyage was nearly unendurable for nineteenth-century refugees and immigrants traveling to America

in steerage. Trapped in a passenger ship's stinking bowels for weeks, suffering the North Atlantic's wind-whipped weather, often seasick, and barely sustained on a diet of often watery soups, these future Americans were robbed of privacy, dignity—truly, any decent comforts.

What courage it must have taken to join such a cavalcade! Yet, a dream sustained them. Simply put, the dream of a better life.[2]

How the immigrants tolerated the terrible voyage in steerage, I do not know. As Dims says, they must have been motivated by "the dream of a better life." Okrent adds more details: ". . . [T]he cost of bringing a passenger to an American port in the cramped, dark, unsanitary steerage compartment of an ongoing ship cost the steamship line $1.70 (2019 equivalent: roughly $55) at a time when the average fare was $22.50 (slightly more than $700 today)."[3] Their trip took ten to twelve days for the crossing, the food was terrible, and steerage was dirty, cramped, and unhealthy. This was what my grandfather endured for the promise of a better a life—I am thankful that he managed it.

My great-grandparents had a second cousin living in New York City. They gave this cousin a little money (my grandfather did not know how much) and asked him to meet their son at the dock when the boat came in and to let him sleep in his apartment. The second cousin agreed.

When David arrived in the United States, the distant cousin met him at the boat, took him home, and let him sleep on the kitchen floor. He also helped David get a job selling candles door to door and later a job in a bakery. The bakery was in the basement of a tenement building, 137 Gorrick Street, in the lower part of Manhattan, in what is now Greenwich Village. The building where my grandfather worked has since been torn down and a new, more luxurious elevator building now stands in its place. The street has been renamed Barrow Street, and Greenwich Village is now a fashionable neighborhood. If you live long enough, you really do see everything.

—

Working in a bakery was a back-breaking job. You had to arrive at five in the morning to make sure that the rolls and bread were available very early so people could have them for breakfast. My grandfather never objected to the long day his work entailed. He kept the bakery open from 5 a.m. to 7 p.m.

As a little girl, I have memories of my mother cautioning my grandfather.

"Papa, stop. Take a minute to rest. You'll get sick," she would say.

He would smile but continue working anyway. By the time the owner of the bakery became ill, my grandfather had saved enough money to buy the business. My grandfather was incredibly entrepreneurial. After buying the bakery, he bought a pushcart (a wagon on wheels) and hired a young boy to deliver rolls in the morning to restaurants in the area, thus making a little extra money. Within a few years he also bought the tenement building in which the bakery was located, and by the age of twenty-seven, he had saved up additional money to go back to the old country and bring his parents and sisters to America. How he saved enough money to do this, I do not know. But I do know that he worked very hard, that he never went out to restaurants or dressed in fancy clothes, and certainly never bought theater tickets or entertained himself in any costly way. He must have been thinking of his mother's words, *Oh, my little David, you will go to America and become a successful American man, and then you will come back and take all of us to America.*

Tragically, when he finally got back to the old country, he learned that his mother had died. The letter informing him of her death had gone astray (this happened often in those days). His father declined to come to America, preferring to stay in the shtetl, where he had spent all his life and where he could remain close to the memory of his wife, but David's two sisters returned to the United States with him. Also, during his trip home, he met a lovely young woman from his community. They were married by the local rabbi, and he brought her back to the States as well. David and his wife had four girls, Flo, Malvina (my mother), Sadie, and Louise, and two boys, Samuel and Julius. David's wife died after giving birth to Julius, their last child. Having children in those years was a dangerous activity.

My mother, Malvina, was very outspoken on every issue, personal and political, and was more or less the leader of her family. Though every one of her siblings made it to middle school (my grandfather made sure of it, as he was a big believer in education, and all the political freedoms that America offered, which were unheard of in the old country), my mother was the only child in her family to go on to high school. She attended two years at Washington Irving High School, and she always regretted not completing her education. Still, she was revered as the most educated member of her family, and no one made any major decisions without consulting her. She and her sister Sadie both worked in the garment district in secretarial positions, but after work my mother always went to the bakery to help my grandfather run his business. She had her father's entrepreneurial spirit and never felt her gender was a barrier when it came to work. The idea of a woman working was no shock to her, and later, I took after her in this way. Indeed, when I was a child, I saw my mother working all the time, and the image of her as independent and industrious has stayed with me all my life.

My mother came into political consciousness in that heady era just after women in the United States won the right to vote, when women began to feel more liberated. This was a fascinating moment in American history, but in order to appreciate it, we need to understand how we got there.

The Nineteenth Amendment, which gave women the right to vote, made a profound difference in the lives of American women and the politics of our nation. As I noted at the beginning of this chapter, the people marching under my window supporting Kamala Harris for the presidency of the United States would certainly have been laughed at and not been allowed to conduct that march before the Nineteenth Amendment was adopted. Before the Nineteenth Amendment, no one could have imagined a presidential election featuring six female candidates, as we have now in 2020.

The adoption of that amendment in 1919 took many decades to achieve. In the middle of the nineteenth century, Susan B. Anthony, Elizabeth Cady Stanton, Lucretia Mott, and a small group of women began to talk about the need for women to have the same rights as men generally and more specifically to be able to vote. The idea of women voting was a radical one in those years. In 1848, after many difficulties, Susan B. Anthony, Elizabeth Cady Stanton, and Lucretia Mott decided to hold what became the first meeting of its kind to discuss women's rights. This meeting became known as the Seneca Falls Convention in New York State, and it was held in July of that year.

On the first day, which was for women only, over 300 women attended. On the second day, men were also invited, and there were almost fifty men in attendance. The declaration that Elizabeth Cady Stanton had drafted included not only a call for political equality but a specific call for the right to vote. Husbands, fathers, and friends of Stanton opposed this section, but Stanton would not remove it. Nothing could make her change her mind.

In 1850, the suffragettes held another convention, and the result of that meeting was that right to vote became an even more important aspect of the movement's goals. Early suffragettes grew old and died, but other young women took their place: Alice Paul and Lucy Burns, to mention just two—women in many ways more militant than Susan B. Anthony and Elizabeth Cady Stanton. They picketed the White House, spent more time in prison, and on March 2, 1913, a day before Wilson's inauguration, they held a parade. The parade didn't go smoothly (a far cry from the march for Kamala)—men watching from the sidelines spit on the women and threatened physical violence, but this and other instances landed their cause on the front pages of the newspapers.

The New York Times, which at first supported women's suffrage, reversed its opinion, and issued a severe warning against it, claiming that if women were free to vote they would "play havoc with it for themselves and society if the men are not firm and wise enough, and, it may well be said, masculine enough to prevent them."[4]

Articles and other magazines predicted that if women voted they would lose their femininity. Most often, pundits stated that politics were dirty, and therefore not suitable for women. But the women persisted and persisted.

World War I also had a profound influence on the women's movement. During the war, many women went overseas with men to serve, not only as nurses, but to drive army vehicles, carry supplies to the front, translate code, type, and do other clerical work—some of it at the front lines. At home, women worked in factories and government office jobs that previously had been done by men. These jobs proved that women could do anything that men could do and certainly earned them the right to vote.

So, after a long struggle, the Nineteenth Amendment was adopted in early 1919. The House passed it by a vote of 304 to 90; the Senate by a vote of 56 to 25. Thirty-six states were needed for ratification. This was achieved by August 18, 1920.

This was how the 1920s began. Not only did women win the right to vote, thus allowing them a voice in the political life of the nation, but this victory heralded the opportunity for women to change the patterns of their lives and adopt a freer lifestyle. These included adjustments to their manners, behavior, and morals. And it was a time when more women worked, which gave them some financial independence, crucial in allowing them to live more fully on their own terms.

Indeed, the Nineteenth Amendment held enormous symbolic power; it opened the door and said women were free to play an active role in the American nation. So-called flappers enjoyed the sense of freedom that the Nineteenth Amendment gave them. During this time, not only did the women dress differently, use makeup, and talk freely with men, but they also enjoyed dancing and all the amenities that their society provided. It was a time of great change for the country and its women.

The same was clearly true for my mother. Once, when my mother was reminiscing about her pre-motherhood days, she confessed that in her youth, she used cosmetics, particularly enjoying lipstick and rouge, and cut her hair into a short bob. She raised her hemlines and gave up her corset. On the occasions that she, my father (who began courting her when she was in high school), and their friends went to Coney Island for a day's outing, she and the other women and men talked openly about many issues including sex. They smoked and drank together. Some of the couples enjoyed premarital sex, but my mother made it clear to me that she was a virgin until she got married. My mother and her sister, Sadie, were part of the new world for women. They always enjoyed the independence that the money they earned from working in the garment district gave them.

My grandfather encouraged my mother's independent mind and ambitions, and she rewarded him with her utmost loyalty. She was my grandfather's favorite, and I know she was particularly helpful to him on Friday night, which was called "Cholent Night" (cholent is a stew made up of various kinds of beans, potatoes, and some "flanken" meat). As is well-known, observant Jews do not cook on Saturdays, and so the cholent was prepared ahead of time so that there would be food to eat when Shabbat was over. On Friday night, many people in the neighborhood would bring their pot of cholent to my grandfather's bakery to be put into the bakery's ovens. Then, they would take their pots out on Saturday night after sundown and eat their dinner from the cholent pot.

Friday night, therefore, was very busy in the bakery with many women and men coming in to put their cholent pots in the ovens. I think my grandfather charged either a nickel or a dime for every pot that was placed in his oven. For poor people, I suspect, he charged nothing.

Late on Friday night, after all the cholent pots were in place in the bakery's oven, my grandfather and all of his children sat down to a family dinner. This tradition continued long into my childhood. We were all of us expected to be in attendance. My father, who had no brothers or sisters, loved my mother's family and would join us at this dinner and at every opportunity he had. My grandfather had hired a housekeeper after the death of his wife, and she shopped and cooked for all of us.

After dinner was served, there were discussions about every-thing—job interviews, the bakery and how it was doing, and American politics. On the final subject, my mother held the floor. She loved talking about politics. This was a trait that stayed with her all her life, and I believe that I became interested in law and politics partially as the result of her influence. She was so much a part of me in so many ways.

My grandfather, too, was very interested in American politics. He could never get over that in America all male citizens were entitled to vote for the people who were going to govern them. "What a wonderful idea!" my grandfather said over and over again. Back in the old country, no one voted for anything, and the emperor made all the decisions and chose all the men around him who were going to carry out those decisions. My grandfather insisted that my mother keep him up to date on the latest developments in American politics. She knew who was running for what office, and from her reports, he learned a great deal about the political landscape in this country.

It was from her, for example, that he learned, a few years before I was born, that a peace conference taking place in Versailles where the countries involved in World War I were struggling to finish the peace treaty. Most Americans, and especially immigrants, had little interest or knowledge about what was happening in Versailles. Unlike them, my grandfather was very interested. Thanks to my mother, my grandfather knew a little bit about the war and that President Woodrow Wilson was in Versailles pleading that a League of Nations be part of the peace treaty. My grandfather thought this league was a great idea.

When Wilson came back to America, he spoke at a public school near where my grandfather's bakery was located. My grandfather, who never took time off from work, took off early that day so he could be in the audience when President Wilson spoke. He agreed with Wilson about a League of Nations, and was dismayed that lots of vacant seats in the auditorium. Most of the immigrants in my grandfather's neighborhood were simply not interested in Wilson's League. They wanted nothing to do with anything that involved Europe's squabbles and felt it was time to let Europe worry about Europe. They only wanted to enjoy the peace and prosperity they earned. My grandfather was sorry for President Wilson and unhappy with the attitude of his immigrant neighbors.

My grandfather thought it was very impressive that Wilson had shepherded the country through the horrors of World War I and was now working with the peace delegates in Versailles in trying to come up with a treaty that would help make the countries of Europe democratic, as well as urging for the creation of a League of Nations.

Though my grandfather admired President Wilson, the twenty-eighth president could not have been more different from my grandfather. Wilson was cold, autocratic, and a brilliant academic. He was a professor and then the president of Princeton University, one of the country's most elitist universities. He was the author of several books on government, politics, and history. He was aloof, very smart, and had very few friends. He was also a stubborn man, who was unable to compromise, a trait that did not help his efforts to get the country to support his League of Nations.

Wilson, however, never gave up on his League. Just as he went to the Lower East Side to make his case, he traveled throughout the country pleading with his countrymen to understand why such a league was critical. It was better, he argued, to try and settle difficult problems between nations around a conference table and not on bloody battlefields. But the country disagreed, and on November 19, 1919, the Congress of the United States rejected the idea of the League of Nations.

By this time, Wilson had had a bad stroke and was almost a prisoner in the White House, being cared for by some personal aides and his wife. You can be sure that his heart was broken at the news of the defeat of the League of Nations, and this added to his illness. Wilson died in February of 1921, and Warren G. Harding was inaugurated as president in March 1921.

Harding could not have been more different than Wilson. He was warm, affable, vulgar, crude, and ignorant about many things, including how the government should function. He liked nothing better than to spend an evening with his "cronies," drinking, playing poker, and gossiping.

Indeed, my grandfather was very glad to have had the chance to see Wilson speak before he died, and he credited my mother and her engagement with the world for granting him this extraordinary experience.

———

My father, Nathan Bronheim, was very different from my socially and politically conscious, engaged, hardworking mother—the Harding to her Wilson, if you will. Still, they came from the same world; they grew up together, and I do believe they understood each other. My father's mother and father had the vegetable store in the tenement building at 137 Gorrick Street, which my mother's father owned. But unlike my mother, my father was not ambitious. He was not enamored with school. He went to high school for about a year and dropped out to look for a job. He was a good looking, charming man. He loved people, music, cards, and jokes. He was the kind of man that people enjoyed spending time with. He pressed my mother to leave high school after two years so they could get married. She agreed. He was twenty-four and she was twenty. He must have been very persuasive, and I believe she loved him. They got married in 1922, and I was born in 1923.

My grandfather was very unhappy with my mother's choice of a husband. As I mentioned earlier, he was particularly attached to my mother. She was his girl, the one who worked with him in the bakery and always helped him. It wasn't just that she talked politics with him endlessly, which he loved, it was that she respected education in the same way he did. My grandfather was shocked that my father had no real regard for education and dropped out of high school after a year. Furthermore, he was critical of my father's inability to hold a job and make enough money to support his family in a decent style.

Indeed, despite his lack of a formal education, my grandfather had earned enough money to buy real estate. He didn't have the money to buy big and fancy buildings on Fifth Avenue or Central Park West. He bought modest buildings mostly in the Bronx and Yonkers. They were simple buildings that did not require a major financial investment. In Europe, Jews were not able to do this and therefore, throughout his life, whenever he could, he bought property.[5] Given his belief in the value of a hard day's work and dedication to my mother, my grandfather just could not understand how my mother married my father. I don't recall any arguments between my mother and my grandfather about my father, but I am sure that in private my grandfather had many conversations with my mother. He thought that an attractive, smart woman like her could certainly have found a different kind of husband.

Nonetheless, my mother was very committed to my father. As newlyweds, my parents first lived at 1515 Boston Road, a building

My parents, Malvina and Nathan Bronheim, during their youth.

that my grandfather had bought in the Bronx. My father hated the Bronx; he missed the Lower East Side, his buddies. There is a tendency today to romanticize the Lower East Side. That is a mistake. Most of the buildings were five story walk-ups with four apartments on each floor and only two shared toilets per floor. The apartments were dark and dreary and because of the toilets in the hall, there was a terrible odor of urine throughout every tenement building. The whole neighborhood was crowded, dirty, and, medically, a disaster. There were few doctors, although through the efforts of groups like the Educational Alliance, some medical assistance was brought into the area. There were bath houses for people to shower and get clean. They could not do this in their own apartments.

In spite of the crowded and unpleasant living quarters, the area was filled with cultural institutions, but most important for my father was the Yiddish theater, which was a prominent part of the Lower East Side. Numerous comedians and actors got their start in that area: Jack Benny, Eddie Cantor, Alan King, and many, many more. My father often complained that he missed the bustling life of his childhood during the periods when we lived in the Bronx.

So, my parents returned to the Lower East Side, moving into my grandfather's apartment. Since my grandfather owned the building, he had merged two apartments, so there was room for my parents and me. After about two years living in my grandfather's apartment, my father had a stable enough job that the family moved into our own apartment, and I began to go to public school.

Still, there was a lot of instability in our lives. In those years, my parents and I moved nearly every year. I'm told that this was not an unusual practice since you received a month's free rent and a paint job when you moved into a new apartment, but to tell the truth, we also had to move for another reason. My father was not always able to pay our rent—he was not, as I have mentioned, exactly a steady worker. In 1926, after my mother and father were married for a few years, my grandfather lent him the money to open a candy store, which my father did, but like all the businesses he tried, he failed. He then went back into sales and sold paper and twine in the garment district and stayed in that area for the rest of his life. When he lost his job, which was frequent, we would have to leave our current apartment and find a smaller, cheaper one. When he got a job again, we moved to a better apartment. Honestly, in my early years, we moved *at least* once a year. This was not unusual for poor immigrants, who also moved regularly depending on the jobs that they held, but it was certainly disruptive to us as a family and very upsetting to my grandfather.

Another misfortune that befell my parents early in their relationship had to do with my mother's health. When I was a baby, my mother started to cough badly, and her doctor thought it might be tuberculosis. In those years, there was no drug to cure this terrifying disease. The only treatment suggested was rest and time in the country where the air was cool and clean. My mother's sister, Flo, was married to a man named Morris Weiss, whose mother owned a boarding house in Mountaindale, near Monticello in New York's Borscht Belt. My mother and her family spent a great deal of time at the boarding house, when they were not at Coney Island. They loved being together and loved being in the country. When the doctor discovered what he thought was tuberculosis, he suggested that my mother remain in the country for a few more months beyond the end of the summer and that my aunts and uncles bring me, a baby of about four or five months, back to New York to take care of me there, leaving my mother to rest in the country.

My Aunt Louise and I when I was
about four months old.

My mother's sisters, Sadie, Flo, and Louise were delighted to take care of me. Even Sam and Julius pitched in. From pictures and reports from my mother and my aunts, I was a smiley, beautiful baby, and I was like a live doll that everyone played with and enjoyed. As I think about my life, I think that perhaps my need to always be surrounded by an "entourage" and my constant desire to have people applauding me was a result of these early days when I was always around admiring people who were non-stop hugging me, kissing me, and praising everything I did. On the other hand, I do not know what price I paid psychologically for being separated from my mother at an early age. I'm sure that played a role in my panic attacks that developed in my later life. In the words of William Wordsworth, "the child is father of the man."

chapter two

My Education in the
Era of Roosevelt

— ✦ —

I do not really have clear memories of my life before I entered high school at the age of twelve. My mother had moved us near Evander Childs High School in the Bronx (away from my father's beloved Lower East Side), hoping that I would go there and not have to travel, but the one friend I had, Hazel, was going to Hunter High School, and I decided I wanted to go with Hazel. My mother was furious and said no. We argued bitterly. My father then entered the discussion, which he rarely did. He mentioned that you had to take a test to get into Hunter High School. He said we should see if I could pass the test before we wasted time arguing about it. As soon as my mother heard you had to take a test and that, therefore, I would be surrounded by smart people, she agreed at once that I should go to Hunter. She always wanted me to be in a place where the education was good and the people around me were smart. It was one of her deepest regrets that she never finished high school, and she not only wanted me to enroll in a good high school, but to go to a place where I was happy and had intelligent schoolmates that I enjoyed, so that I would be motivated to stay in school until I graduated.

My mother was right: My experience at Hunter High School was wonderful. I received a great education, surrounded by intelligent students and faculty. There is no doubt that my education there furnished the foundation for my future. It was probably one of the most important periods of my life.

Up until then, I had attended regular public school on the Lower East Side and in the Bronx, and, as a result, my life was very limited. Everyone around me was a poor Jew. At Hunter, I met Black people, Christians, poor people, and rich people. My two best friends at Hunter High were Aileen Austin and Peggy Lightfoot. They were very, very rich. Aileen lived on 88th Street and Madison Avenue, and Peggy lived on the eastern end of 86th Street near the East River. Both of their fathers were in advertising. Peggy's father created Father's Day. When I visited their apartments, I couldn't believe my eyes.

Aileen had her own bedroom and bathroom, something unheard of in my world in the Bronx. In my apartment, David, my younger brother, had the bedroom, and I slept in the hall on a couch. We had one bathroom for the entire family (and that was an upgrade from the cramped living quarters of the Lower East Side). In Aileen's house, her sister also had her own bedroom and her own bathroom. There was also a maid's room the size of David's bedroom. There was even a doorman who announced you when entered the building. Peggy's apartment was basically the same with even more rooms and more bathrooms overlooking the East River. Both Peggy and Aileen were not Jewish, but it didn't matter—we were inseparable.

Looking back, I think that ever since then I have had an inner desire to live like Aileen and Peggy, and that came, in some part, from that early exposure to their apartments. Even though my husband Leonard and I were never really rich, our apartment when we were first married was in Riverdale, a very beautiful area, then we lived in Hastings, then moved to Manhattan at 415 West End Avenue, and then to 451 West End Avenue where we lived for twenty-five years. At 451 West End Avenue, there was a doorman, two bedrooms, two bathrooms, and a maid's room with its own bathroom—just like Aileen's childhood apartment. The apartment had a huge living room with a fireplace. Still, one of its most important features was that it was one block from Zabar's, the great Jewish deli, when Zabar's was a small, cramped store squeezed between a dry cleaner and an SRO hotel.

Though Peggy and Aileen were my best friends, I had many others, too, and I never felt lonely or bored in that period of my life. It was then, that, like my mother, I became very interested in politics, law, and government. I was active in the student council and for the first time began to speak publicly at meetings. In the beginning, I was shy about public speaking, but, with practice, I overcame my fear. I was even elected president of the student council in my junior year. I had a marvelous teacher, Ms. Gunther, who taught a course called the Principles of Democracy, which included not only an analysis the Constitution and the American legal system, but also an introduction to the tenets that made for democratic government and those that led to fascism. While I came into Hunter wanting to be a doctor, after a year or so of Ms. Gunther's lectures, I decided that I wanted to be a teacher, just like her. I dreamed of being a history teacher in the city's high schools—history was my passion.

Joking around with a friend at Hunter High School.

This may have been an exciting period in my life, but they were frightening and difficult years throughout the world. The Great Depression and the Second World War weighed heavily on the American psyche, the latter especially heavily on the minds of American Jews. The lessons I learned about the principles of democracy spoke directly to the horrific conflict raging in Europe, which cast a long shadow over our lives.

Indeed, the great economic boom that lasted throughout the 1920s came to a devastating end early in my childhood. The Roaring Twenties, the decade following World War I, was a time of wealth and excess. Building on postwar optimism, rural Americans migrated to the cities in vast numbers throughout the decade with the hopes of finding a more prosperous life thanks to the ever-growing expansion of the American industrial sector. No one seemed to believe that any business could fail. Investors kept purchasing millions of dollars' worth of stocks, which drove the prices higher and higher. This rise in prices gave the appearance of great business profits, and new millionaires were made every day. More and more Americans started buying stocks, often investing their lifetime savings. Most stock market investors were buying on credit, or on margin as it is called in the stock market, borrowing from their stockbrokers, who usually gave them large amounts of credit. Investors expected that they would get rich quick. The market was filled with speculators. To stem the tide, economists called on the Federal Reserve Board (the Fed) to raise interest rates. The Fed raised interest rates twice, but it had no effect.

There were signs throughout this period indicating that there might be trouble ahead, but no one seemed to be paying any attention. Foolish exuberance increased the purchases of stock to a point where speculation was doomed. The bankers had also loaned a lot of money to help farmers purchase the equipment they needed, and when those farmers could not repay the banks, the banks began to fail.

What happened next is well-known in broad strokes, but the statistics are striking. During the Depression thirteen million people became unemployed. Between 1929 and 1932, industrial production fell by nearly 45 percent, home building dropped by 80 percent, about 5,000 banks went out of business, the US GDP fell 30 percent, and the Stock Market lost almost 90 percent of its value—all in *three years.*

So, where was the government in all this? The Republicans who were in power were, as usual, primarily interested in the promotion of business, tax reduction, and high tariffs. As part of President Harding's program to stimulate business, he turned to the customary Republican task of raising the tariff. Little was done to help the unemployed, many of whom were starving. In. sum, the government made no real efforts to help them.

While the problems began in the 1920s, their full effect became more apparent as time moved on into the 1930s. Prices began to shrink. Business fell off. Factories and mines shut down. Agriculture lay prostrate. Commercial banks that failed totaled 28,000 with liabilities of more than $1.52 billion. Among their number was the largest bank failure in US history: the Bank of the United States located in New York City. Before the run on it began it held deposits of $200 million.

Here's what happened precisely: In September 1929, prices in the Stock Market began to drop steadily. Prices continued to drop throughout October until the twenty-fourth, the day that became known as Black Thursday. That morning, a flood of selling began on the floor of the New York Stock Exchange. It is generally believed that brokers started the wave of selling because they needed cash to pay back their loans. When investors saw stock prices dropping, they started selling too. The floor of the Stock Exchange was soon in a panic. By midday, the prices of many stocks were half of what they had been the day before. The more prices plummeted, the more investors sold off their stock. At 12:30 p.m., the exchange closed its visitors' gallery. Outside the building a huge crowd gathered on Wall Street. The Stock Exchange had already lost $4.1 billion. That afternoon, some of the nation's most powerful bankers, including JP Morgan, met to try to stem the tide. Many of them had their fortunes tied up in the stock market. The bankers decided to pool $40 million and buy stock. They hoped that the influx of money would stabilize prices so that investors would stop selling. The strategy worked for a couple of days and the market settled down, but on Tuesday, October 29, the selling frenzy began again. This time the bankers did not come to the rescue. On Black Tuesday, more than sixteen million shares of stock were sold. By the end of the day many stocks were virtually worthless. Altogether stock prices declined by over $10 billion. Entire fortunes were wiped out and many millionaires became penniless overnight.

By the end of 1929, stockholders had lost $40 billion in the stock market crash, but that was just the beginning. It was the most calamitous stock market crash in the history of the United States, and it signaled the start of a twelve-year Great Depression that affected all western industrialized countries. Not only the holdings of stock, not only the banks, not only in business, but all of America, all of the western world, suffered. And for the most part the Republicans stood still.

Companies now had no money to conduct business, so they laid off workers. Within four months more than four million Americans were unemployed. Thousands of companies went out of business because many Americans did not have the money to buy their goods or services. Unemployment rose to eight million by mid 1931. and then skyrocketed to 13.5 million by the end of that year. About one-third of the entire American workforce was out of work. Just think—13.5 million people had no jobs and income.

As hunger and starvation became ever-more serious problems, bread lines formed filled with people waiting for free handouts of soup and bread from charities. Many Americans lost their homes when they could not pay their monthly mortgage installments. A new homeless population constructed huts out of cardboard and moved into city parks and built campfires to stay warm. These little villages were called "Hoovervilles." Others fought over scraps of food that they found in garbage cans. Some wandered the country as hobos, searching desperately for any work at all. One estimate put the number of drifters in America in 1931 at one million, with 100,000 of them children in New York City. A dramatic symbol of the Depression appeared as 6,000 apple sellers set up stands on the streets and tried to survive by selling apples for five cents each.

To make matters worse, the United States of the early 1920s and 1930s had no government social programs to ease the hardships. There was no unemployment insurance, no Social Security, no Medicare, nor were there food stamps. The only help available was from local governments and charities such as the Red Cross and the Salvation Army. Unfortunately, they too began to run out of money by the end of 1931. The mood of America was so hopeless that the birth rate dropped for the first time in many years as people put off having children they could not afford. The country was as close to a revolution as any country can be. Thankfully, in 1932, the country chose Franklin Delano Roosevelt as its leader.

———

Many names have been given to the decade between 1920 and 1930. It has been called the Flapper Age, the Decade of Prohibition, the Age of the Teapot Scandals, and the Women's March to Freedom, to mention just a few. But there is only one name that should be given to the period between 1930 to 1940 and that is Franklin Delano Roosevelt (FDR). I really believe that without FDR and the laws he enacted in his first hundred days, we may very well have seen our nation slide into revolution and become a communist or socialist country. The number of these laws and the innovation that many of them contained is extraordinary. They used novel approaches to try and solve the issues that were destroying our nation. FDR and his associates were faced with some of the most difficult questions, such as:

- What kind of laws were needed to save the banks?
- What kind of program would put money in the hands of the farmers?
- What kind of legislation could put 13 million people back to work as soon as possible?
- What kinds of programs could help musicians, artists, writers, and actors, all of whom needed support?
- How could one develop a social security plan to help the elderly that was workable and which the country could afford?

These are only a few of the questions that Roosevelt and the men and women around him tried to answer. In some cases, they were successful, in others they were not, but the group around Roosevelt was an exceptional group. At no other time in our history has anything matched this. It is worth discussing some of these measures in greater detail, as they altered my life and the lives of millions of Americans.

Within thirty-six hours of taking office, FDR issued two proclamations: one declaring an official bank holiday throughout the country, and the other calling on Congress to come to Washington at once. On March 9, Congress convened for a session that lasted a hundred days. With FDR pressing them incessantly, the Congress enacted a series of very important laws with breathtaking speed that gave Roosevelt the beginning of his New Deal.

The first item that Roosevelt tackled in the first hundred days was the crisis of the banks. As I said before, more than 5,000 banks were in the process of being closed. Imagine if you could not get your life savings out of the bank because it was closed. People were very panicked about this.

Roosevelt called his secretary of the treasury, William Woodin, to come up with some solution. During the bank holiday, he met with the governors of each of the states, members of the banking community, and the press. Roosevelt was an astute politician, and he knew that he could only get his New Deal legislation passed if he had the support of political leaders, the press, and the public. He understood how important the press was in reaching the public, and he never left them out of any important decisions.

Secretary Woodin came up with an idea. He suggested that the Federal Reserve Board issue new currency that would be backed not by gold or silver but by the assets in the banks in the Federal Reserve System. Roosevelt approved the plan at once. The act also authorized the secretary of the treasury to review and reopen all the banks that were found to be solvent and reorganize those that were in trouble.

The entire legislative process for the enactment of this bill took less than six hours. Those banks approved by the secretary of the treasury received a license to reopen. As the biographer Jean Edward Smith stated succinctly in his book about FDR, "within a month, eight out of every ten banks were open again."[1] You can imagine the joy Americans experienced when they finally felt their savings were secure.

Since the plight of the farmer was a major cause of the Depression, Roosevelt next turned his attention to raising the income of the farmers by reducing crop surpluses. Under the bill he proposed, the government would pay the farmers *not* to produce crops beyond an amount set by the Department of Agriculture. Farmers would get immediate income through these allotment payments. By restricting the number of crops grown, produce prices were expected to rise.

It was a radical idea, but FDR pointed out that desperate situations demanded new and radical ideas. Funding for the allotment payments would come from a tax on millers, canners, packers, textile manufacturers, among others. Roosevelt saw this program as critical to his New Deal. Like his other new and inventive ideas, it gave the desperate farmers ready cash—something they badly needed.

After working on the banking and the agricultural crisis, Roosevelt turned his attention to putting men to work through the Civilian Conservation Corps (CCC) Act. This program did two things: it put men to work, and it helped the environment by funding projects that fought soil erosion and protected natural resources. The men planted trees, cared for seedlings, built bridges, dug reservoirs, and worked on flood control. Men aged 18–25 lived in government-built camps, and they received food, clothing, and $1 a day, or $30 a month, $25 of which they had to send home. Enlistment was for six months with the possibility of renewals for up to two years.

It worked like this: The Department of Labor recruited the men; the Army ran the camps; and the Forest Service supervised the work. Labor voiced objections to the plan at first, as they felt the $1 a day would depress wages. They complained, too, that life in the camps sounded too regimented. FDR met at once with representatives of Labor. He did not back down and managed to soften their criticism.

The bill was adopted, although Labor continued to be unhappy with it. Nonetheless, it proved to be one of FDR's most popular programs. He asked for and received $500 million from Congress for the program. By the time the United States entered World War II, the CCC had put more than three million men to work and saved scores of forests. FDR was always very proud of this program. It was his idea and reflected his lifelong interest in conservation.

But this was not all. In fact, this was just the beginning. Next FDR cooked up the National Industrial Recovery Act, which was the most ambitious legislation of the hundred days. As Smith writes in *FDR*:

On April 6 the Senate, acting on its own initiative, passed a bill (53–30) introduced by Senator Hugo Black of Alabama that would bar from interstate commerce goods produced in plants where employees worked more than five days a week or six hours a day. By limiting the workweek to thirty hours, Black and his supporters claimed, the bill would create six million new jobs.

FDR was caught off guard. He believed the Black bill was unconstitutional, that it was inflexible, and that it would retard recovery by forcing employers into a straitjacket. But with the vigorous support of organized labor, the bill appeared unstoppable.[2]

In response, Roosevelt, working with his labor secretary, Frances Perkins, and secretary of war, George Dern, created a more extensive bill than the Black Bill. He sent this new bill to the Congress on May 17. Title 1 of that bill authorized businesses to establish production codes controlling prices and output in each industry free from antitrust regulation. Another section of the bill guaranteed labor's right to bargain collectively and stipulated that the industry codes should set minimum wages and maximum hours. Another section contained Roosevelt's public works proposal: $3.3 billion in government spending.

The House approved the bill with a wide majority in favor. The Senate was more divided. Progressive lawmakers were concerned about the leeway granted to businesses to set prices and production levels; conservatives were not pleased about the provisions that protected collective bargaining for labor. But, ultimately, centrist voices won out, and the Senate ultimately approved the bill.

This bill created the Public Works Administration (PWA), which oversaw programs that were not only involved in physical construction, but in providing work in art, music, theater, and white-collar jobs. Free concerts and plays afforded entertainment for vast numbers of people—all done under the auspices of the PWA.

Between 1933 and 1939, more than one million Americans found work through the PWA, which completed more than 35,000 projects, including the construction of highways, hospitals, bridges, dams, universities, and waterworks. The PWA also built more than 20,000 units of low-cost housing, which charged only $26 a month for rent. In the big cities, PWA workers tore down the worst slums and built affordable apartment buildings.

This was an extraordinary piece of legislation, and I'd like to pause for a moment to discuss the woman who crafted it. So, a word on Frances Perkins, whose name I have mentioned above a few times. As I noted, Perkins was Roosevelt's secretary of labor. She was the first woman in a cabinet position. The Public Works Bill was not her only legacy. She was particularly crucial in the passing of social security in the years to come. The idea was hers and she worked tirelessly to get it done. She also played a critical role in fighting for unemployment insurance, child labor laws, and the forty-hour work week. Ultimately, she was Roosevelt's "Idea Lady." We owe a great deal to her. Unfortunately most people have forgotten about her today. Nonetheless, we live with her legacy, and our nation is the better for her service.

It is important to note, though, that not everything FDR and his team did in those first 100 days was a rousing triumph. For example, the National Recovery Administration (NRA), which Roosevelt considered one of his most important programs, was not a success. The NRA tried to encourage labor and management to work cooperatively. Roosevelt thought it would be helpful if large corporations worked together to set standards for production and prices. This required the NRA to suspend the antitrust laws. Businesses were also required to establish codes on competition and fair labor standards. The government only licensed businesses that agreed to a minimum wage and limited work hours. Workers were given the right to choose their own unions and organize for collective bargaining. Efforts to break up unions were outlawed. The NRA failed. The codes wound up restricting business rather than encouraging it.

Still, the New Deal was one of the most impressive political feats of the past century. And it was hardly the only matter on Roosevelt's mind during his first term. While FDR was pushing his New Deal legislation, he was also concerned about the budget. He felt that salaries of government workers and benefits given to veterans after World War I were too high. He wanted to cut the salaries of government employees by 15 percent. Congressional pay would be reduced from $10,000 to $8,000 and his own salary from $90,000 to $75,000. You can imagine the critical outcry this produced—not only from his enemies, but from his friends. After lots of meetings and compromises, a budget bill incorporating much of what FDR wanted was passed. This is a dramatic example of Roosevelt's political savvy. To get Congress to cut its own salaries required a politician with near magical abilities, and Roosevelt apparently had such skill.

In our home, we adored FDR, and, as you can tell, my admiration for the great politician has never wavered. Whenever there was a fireside chat being broadcast, we would listen. We never missed it. To us, the president seemed friendly; he had a tone that was confident and assured. He gave us the feeling that he was going to beat the Depression and get our country moving again—words we all sorely needed to hear. I can still hear it today, the president's happy and confident voice, assuring us that everything was going to be okay.

I could spend many more pages discussing the many important programs FDR instituted, but I want to speak about one that touched my life directly. It would not have been possible for me to go to law school without it. To earn money during my time as a law student, I worked in the library at Columbia Law School. My job was part of a New Deal Program, directed by the Works Progress Administration (WPA), called the National Youth Administration. The purpose of this youth organization was to help keep high school and college students stay in school. The government ensured that students were paid up to $30 a month for jobs in their schools. They could work as library clerks, tutors, typists, and so on. So, the work I did, checking the books that were returned or not returned, keeping stacks up to date and clean, and writing notes to students who kept their books out too long, all that was paid for by FDR's genius. Without the money I made in this fashion, I would have had difficulty staying at the Columbia Law School.

But I'm getting ahead of myself. We're not there yet. There's more to tell. I have to explain how I got to Columbia Law School in the first place.

My mother, as I have mentioned, always emphasized the importance of education, as her father had done with her, and so, to her credit, she never suggested that I go and get a job after high school in order to support us. She absolutely encouraged me to go to college. Our family needed the money, but she was clear, education came first.

So, after graduating Hunter High School, I went on to Hunter College, as did many of my classmates. There was no fuss about getting into Hunter College for anyone who graduated with decent grades from Hunter High. It was a natural step forward. I continued my subway rides from the Bronx. Hunter High was on 96th Street and Hunter College on 68th Street, a difference of a few stops. At the college, I made some new friends, but I also carried with me some of the friends I made in high school. While I loved college, these were also dark times. I was extremely concerned with what Hitler was doing over in Europe and scared to death that if he ever won Jews like me would all be killed.

But first, I must back up a little, to explain how Hitler came to power in the first place, and what he was doing that was so frightening to us all.

Adolf Hitler was born in Austria, which was then part of the Austro-Hungarian Empire. He moved to Germany in 1913 and was decorated for his service in the German army in World War I.

In 1919, he joined the German Workers' Party, and then two years later, in 1921 formed the Nazi Party. In 1923, he attempted to seize power in a failed coup in Munich and was imprisoned. In jail, he wrote the first volume of his autobiography and political manifesto, *Mein Kampf*—a deeply antisemitic text that blamed Jews for most of Germany's problems. After being released in 1924, he gained popular support by attacking the Treaty of Versailles and promoting pan-Germanism, antisemitism, and anti-communism. He was a charismatic orator and a genius at propaganda. He frequently denounced international capitalism and Communism as part of a Jewish conspiracy. His ideas struck a chord with many German people who were living with the crushing terms of the Versailles Treaty and had endured a horrible depression for years.

Indeed, he was so successful at convincing the German people that By November 1932, the Nazi party had the most seats in the German Reichstag. Still, they did not have a majority, and no party was able to form a majority parliamentary coalition in support of a candidate for the chancellorship. A former chancellor, Franz von Papen, and other conservative leaders persuaded the president to appoint Hitler as Chancellor in 1933.

Hitler had no qualms making it clear, in both speeches and writings, that he planned to eliminate Jews from Germany and any country that he conquered. He spoke frequently about establishing a new order in Europe to counter what he saw as the injustice of the post–World War I international order dominated by Britain and France. He also believed Britain and France were influenced by the Jews and blamed the horrific economic conditions in

Germany on the Jews. In the face of these bald lies, Germany and the rest of Europe were mostly silent.

Now that he had attained power through legal measures, Hitler moved very quickly to expand it. In February 1933, Hitler suspended all civil liberties after the German parliament (the Reichshtag) caught fire. A Dutch Communist was convicted of the crime, but some believed the Nazis did it themselves as a ploy to create chaos and increase their influence. Indeed, Hitler did exactly that. In March, he called for new elections. The Nazis won control of the government, and Hitler gained the authority to decree laws.

In April 1933, Hitler dismissed all Jewish office holders and mandated a boycott of Jewish businesses. When mobs attacked Jews and their shops throughout Germany, local authorities did nothing. In May 1933, Hitler outlawed unions and sent union leaders to work-prisons, called concentration camps. By the end of the year, he made the Nazi Party the only legal political party in the country and withdrew Germany from the League of Nations. In violation of the Treaty of Versailles, he also began a massive rebuilding of Germany's military. On June 30, 1934, known as the Night of the Long Knives (a phrase from a popular Nazi song), Hitler had nearly two hundred opponents within the Nazi Party murdered and said it was "in self-defense of the state." In August, when Paul von Hindenberg died, Hitler assumed the presidency. He was now the absolute dictator of Germany.

Meanwhile, Hitler continued to rebuild the military, threaten neighboring countries, and oppress the Jews. In March 1935, Hitler announced the creation of an army of 500,000 men through mandatory military service. In September 1935, he instituted the Nuremberg Laws, which stripped Jews of their German citizenship and outlawed marriages between Jews and so-called Aryans. In March 1936, Hitler made his first military move by occupying the Rhineland, an area of Germany bordering France that had been deemed a permanently demilitarized zone by the

Treaty of Versailles. In October 1936, Hitler formed the Rome–Berlin Axis Coalition, an alliance with Italy's Mussolini after the Italians' conquest of Ethiopia.

Later, in November 1936, Japan signed a pact with Germany and became the third nation in the Axis Powers. Both Germany and Japan agreed to consult on issues concerning the Soviet Union and support each other in case of a Soviet attack. Japan's military had used the depression as an excuse to take control of the Japanese government in 1930 and subsequently began their own program of conquest and expansion in China. From 1931-32, Japan took control of Manchuria in China. The League of Nations condemned the invasion but had no power to prevent it. In 1933, Japan withdrew from the League of Nations. Now these three autocatic and expansionist powers, Japan, Italy, and Germany, were allied against the democratic world.

Indeed, in 1938, Hitler revealed his intention to "defend the rights" of the German people (a phony excuse) living in the bordering countries of Austria and Czechoslovakia. European leaders knew that this was a threat to invade those two countries and unify them with Germany. Even so, no one really tried to stop him.

In Czechoslovakia, Hitler was focused on the Sudetenland, a province on the Czech-German border that was mostly inhabited by Germans who supported Hitler. In Austria, Hitler also had support among the ethnically German Austrians, who desired reunification with Germany, a union forbidden by the Treaty of Versailles. Hitler eventually demanded that Austrian leader Chancellor Kurt von Schuschnigg give more power to German Austrian Nazis in the Austrian government. Schuschnigg agreed but then tried to settle the issue once and for all by calling for a vote of all Austrians, asking them whether they wanted to remain independent or join Germany. Hitler did not wait for the results of the vote. German troops invaded Austria on March 12, meeting little resistance. The next day, Hitler announced that Austria had been annexed. It was now a part of Germany.

Britain and France accepted the announcement knowing that war would have been the only way to stop him. This acceptance, or appeasement, of Hitler's actions avoided immediate war, but it also made Hitler believe he could get away with his demands without real opposition.

With Austria in hand, Hitler next turned his sights on Czechoslovakia and the Sudetenland. First, he positioned his troops on the Czech border in a clear preparation for invasion. The military buildup resulted in a series of negotiations, mostly between Hitler and British Prime Minister Neville Chamberlain, during which Hitler demanded that the Sudetenland be granted to Germany. The situation was particularly alarming because both Britain and France had promised to defend the Czech border militarily. In a final meeting between Hitler and Chamberlain in Munich on September 29, 1930, Chamberlain agreed to cede the Sudetenland in return for Hitler's promise that there would be no more territorial demands. The appeasement came to be known as the Munich Agreement. Chamberlain returned home to Britain saying the result was "peace in our time." Many others knew this agreement spelled disaster. Hitler was not through with his demands. Hitler never meant peace under any conditions and his promises were worthless. Most thinking people understood this—not Chamberlain.

Meanwhile, while the world watched Europe in horror, FDR kept a close watch on Japan, as well. In July 1937, Japan used a small clash between Japanese and Chinese civilians near the Manchurian border to justify a full invasion of China. In August 1937, Japan occupied Beijing, then called Peking, and later set up a puppet government controlled by Japan. In November, Shanghai fell to Japanese troops after the Chinese army lost 270,000 troops defending the city. In December 1937, Japanese troops occupied Nanking and sank an American gun boat in a convoy of oil tankers, killing three Americans and injuring forty-three. A major conflict with the US was averted when the Japanese government apologized to America and agreed to pay damages. However, the occupation of Nanking came to be called the Rape of Nanking after an estimated two hundred thousand people were murdered and twenty thousand women and girls were raped by Japanese troops. Throughout 1938, Japanese troops pushed deeper into China from the north and east and easily defeated the untrained Chinese troops. In an act of desperation in June 1938, Chinese forces opened the dikes of the Yellow River allowing the river to flood. The flood halted the advance of Japanese troops, but it also killed many Chinese civilians who lived in the area. By the end of the year, the Chinese leader had withdrawn his troops into the mountains and Japan occupied most of eastern China.

At the same time, the persecution of Jews in Nazi Germany also reached a crisis stage. After the annexation of Austria, the Nazis began sending most Jews to concentration camps. At the time, the camps were really prisons where prisoners performed forced labor, often dying from mistreatment. Later the camps were used to kill Jews through outright murder by shooting them and putting them in mass graves or burning them in crematories. In October, the Nazis confiscated the property of about 12,000 Polish Jews living in Germany and deported them. Ten days after the deportation, the son of one of the Polish families shot and killed a German diplomat in Paris. On November 10, throughout Germany the Nazis organized what they called "demonstrations" against the Jews out of retribution for the assassination. The demonstrations turned violent, as planned, and thousands of Jewish homes, synagogues, and shops were attacked and were destroyed. An estimated ninety-one Jews were killed, and many others were injured on a night that came to be known as Kristallnacht, or the "Night of the Broken Glass." The next day, the Nazi government claimed that the Jews were responsible for the destruction on that night and arrested 20,000 to be sent to the concentration camps. All of Germany's remaining 500,000 Jews were fined a billion marks to pay for the damages, payable to the German government. There was no response from Britain or France. In Washington, Roosevelt granted permits to 15,000 German and Austrian refugees, mostly Jews, allowing them into the United States. No country, except the United States, cried out in response to the tragedy facing the Jews.

As was to be expected, foreign policy dominated Roosevelt's presidency in 1939, for the first time since he took office. By the end of 1938, he was certain the US would not be able to avoid being part of the war that was clearly coming. Roosevelt had reluctantly signed the Neutrality Act, which had been passed by Congress in 1935 and forbade commerce or the transport of American weapons to any nation involved in a war. He now strongly opposed the measure, but isolationists controlled Congress and spoke for the majority of Americans. People were reluctant to fight another war after World War I. Nonetheless, in December 1938, Roosevelt approved the secret sale of 1,000 airplanes to France. Two weeks, later during his State of the Union Address, he again warned of the dangers of isolationism. He also asked for more money for national defense and a revision of the Neutrality Act. Several more developments in Europe would have to take place before Congress finally agreed.

These began in March, when Hitler completed the occupation of Czechoslovakia by sending German and Hungarian troops into the remaining provinces. In April, Italy conquered Albania, putting Italian troops in a position to invade Greece. Britain and France again accepted these occupations, but Britain's Prime Minister Chamberlain finally realized Hitler's intentions and swore to militarily defend the independence of Poland, Greece, and Romania.

On the other side of the globe, throughout early 1939, Japan continued its conquest of China. By March, Japan controlled Hainan, an island province in the southeast of China from which naval invasions of neighboring countries, such as the Philippines, could easily be launched.

Then, in August the Allies suffered a surprising blow. The Soviet Union and its leader Joseph Stalin, who was thought to be a potential ally against the Axis countries, signed a nonaggression pact with Hitler's Germany. The two countries promised no military action against each other for ten years. The real purpose of the pact was even more threatening and kept secret. The two leaders both agreed to invade Poland and split the country between them. Germany would also claim Lithuania, while the Soviet Union was granted Finland, Latvia, and Estonia. Thus, by mid-1939, Nazi Germany, the Soviet Union, fascist Italy, and Japan were carrying out plans for world conquest while all other nations stood by. The isolationists in America stood firm throughout all of these developments. There was a debate in Congress about amending the Neutrality Act, but there was little support for the plan, and Congress adjourned in August 1939. Roosevelt was able to terminate a 1911 treaty with Japan in which the United States supplied Japan with huge amounts of steel and other materials used for building ships and weapons. Otherwise, he could do little but issue official statements of protest. Roosevelt also sent personal messages to Hitler and Mussolini, including a list of thirty-three European and Middle Eastern countries that he wanted them to pledge not to invade. The two dictators ridiculed Roosevelt's request.

On September 1, 1939, just one week after Germany and the Soviet Union signed the nonaggression pact, German troops stormed into Poland. Two days later, Britain and France each declared war on Germany, and World War II began. That same day, a German submarine sank the British ship *Athenia* off the coast of Scotland, killing one hundred and twelve people, including twenty-eight Americans. According to the Neutrality Act, which denied protection to Americans who were traveling on ships of nations at war, the Americans were traveling beyond the protection of the US government, so no action was taken in response.

On September 17, 1939, Soviet Union troops attacked Poland from the west. Britain and France decided not to send troops to Poland, but mobilized their militaries in France, anticipating a German invasion there. Alone the Polish army was no match for either the German or Soviet invading forces. Some of the Polish soldiers fought on horseback with lances instead of guns. On September 28, Warsaw, the Polish capital, surrendered, and Poland was divided between Germany and Russia, just as Hitler and Stalin had agreed one month earlier. In late September, Roosevelt called Congress into session to revise the Neutrality Act. Despite the invasion of Poland, isolationism remained strong in the United States. Roosevelt, however, had new support to reverse the act. First, it was clear that the US embargo against selling arms to the countries at war was only hurting the Allies. Germany's military strength was far superior to Britain and France. Also, the American people were changing their minds. They still did not want US troops involved, but polls showed that eighty-four percent wanted the Allies to win and just two percent favored the Axis Powers. Sixty percent favored the repeal of the Neutrality Act.

On November 3, 1939, Congress passed a revised Neutrality Act ending the arms embargo. Americans could now sell arms to warring nations, as long as they were paid for in cash, not through loans or gifts, and not transported by US ships. To satisfy the isolationists who thought that incidents such as the *Athenia* attack would bring the US into the war, Americans were forbidden from traveling on the ships of warring nations or to enter their ports. Not only did the lifting of the arms embargo aid the Allies, but arms production also proved to be the economic spark that lifted the US economy out of the Depression.

After Poland's surrender in late September, Germany sat tight. Germany's inaction led some isolationists in the US to call the crisis the "phony war." Hitler called for a peace conference, but the Allies responded that talks could only take place after Nazi troops were removed from Poland. The Allies suspected the call for a peace conference was one of Hitler's tricks, and this time they were right. Hitler was actually stalling for time, while he planned the invasion of France. The invasion had been scheduled for November 1939, but France had one of Europe's largest armies, and in addition 158,000 British troops had joined them. Hitler would need the winter of 1939–40 to build up his military.

There was fighting, however, as the Soviet Union invaded Finland, a country that had been under Russian rule until 1917. As the European war expanded in 1939, the Soviet Union wanted more protection for their important port in Leningrad near the Finland-Russia border. The Soviet Union proposed a trade of lands, changing Finland's boundaries but Finland refused. On November 30, 1939, the Soviet Union invaded Finland, an attack that included airstrikes on civilians in Helsinki. British and French troops again remained in France. Roosevelt quickly denounced the invasion, and a bill was introduced in Congress to loan Finland $60 million to buy arms. By the time the bill was passed, isolationists had reduced it to $20 million for food. Without military assistance Finland could not overcome the Soviet Union, and the Fins found themselves under Soviet rule by March 19, less than four months after the invasion began.

Meanwhile, Hitler was planning a spring invasion of France followed by an air invasion of England. In December, he received assurances from Major Vidkun Quisling, a Nazi sympathizer in the Norwegian Army, that Quisling was planning a military coup in Norway and would help Germany occupy his Scandinavian nation. The Axis powers were meeting little resistance in their plans for world conquest.

In America, President Roosevelt had finally received the authority to sell arms to the Allies but there were few arms to sell. The Depression and strong isolationism had brought arms production in American to a standstill. This was a major problem because, as time marched on, so did Hitler's troops. After the conquest of Poland, Hitler conquered country after country in Europe, including Romania, Austria, Hungary, small and large countries in the Balkans, Denmark, Belgium, the Netherlands, and France.

The German conquest of France was a particular heartache for the millions of people for whom France stood as the symbol of democracy in Europe. With France's fall, democracy no longer existed on continental Europe. The island nation of Britain stood alone. This disaster was devastating for me just as it was for every other person committed to the concept of democratic government.

After conquering all of Europe, Germany began its air war against Britain. Germany started first by bombing British airfields. Then on Hitler's orders, the Nazi air force began bombing Liverpool and London. This was a tactical error on Hitler's part, as it gave the British air force time to repair their airplanes which had been damaged by the Nazi air force.

Still, hundreds of British men, women, and children died in the air war in London and Liverpool, but the British fought bravely to save their country. And they did. The airplanes that the United States sent to Britain during this time clearly helped her defeat the German planes and spared Britain the loss of her country. The British royal family stayed in London during the attack by the German planes. The British people respected them for this, and it helped in developing a warm and trusting relationship between the royal family and the British people. Whatever he could do to help the British, Roosevelt did. And while the bravery of the British was indisputably the reason Britain survived, the help from the United States was also of great importance.

While Hitler was conquering Europe and killing and imprisoning Jews in concentration camps, Americans were still largely isolationists, although the polls showed that they had increasing support for the Allies. But their support for the Allies did not minimize their determination to stay out of Europe's squabbles.

Roosevelt repeated his pledge to keep "our boys" out of this war, but more and more, in his heart, he supported the British. Roosevelt had the idea of to give Britain destroyers, which they needed badly, in exchange for Britain offering the United States some naval bases in the Caribbean and off the coast of Canada on which the United States could build military installations. This plan did not need Congressional approval, and so as a result, Roosevelt was able to do it and the United States sent fifty destroyers to Britain.

The Lend-Lease Act was another of Roosevelt's innovative ideas to help the British without explicitly entering the war. Under this proposal, the United States would lend the British the armaments, food, and other supplies, including military supplies, that they needed to survive. The British did not have to pay for these items on receipt, but at the end of the war they would then be required to pay either in goods, money, or services. The Lend-Lease Act managed to pass both houses of Congress, and President Roosevelt signed it into law on March 12, 1941.

Still, on the question of the destruction of European Jewry, by and large, the American public remained silent. Rabbi Stephen Wise, president of the American Jewish Congress at the time, was one of the few people in the country who did speak out. He organized a major rally at Madison Square Garden (attended by 80,000 people) that decried what Hitler was doing to the Jews and other people in Europe, but, still, the United States did nothing, the rest of the world did nothing, and six million Jews were systematically exterminated, and Hitler continued to conquer Europe.

Even if Roosevelt increasingly thought that it would be impossible to avoid entering the conflict, he was also very concerned that our country was not ready to get into a war. We had only a few soldiers and most of our equipment was old and left over from World War I. As a result, he pressed very hard for the Selective Training and Service Act, a draft that required all men between the ages of eighteen and thirty-five to serve in the Army for two years. In 1940, Congress passed the law. Never before had there been a draft in peacetime in our history. The isolationists were furious.

While Europe was in flames, Roosevelt was also keeping an eye on what was happening in Japan. The US refused to recognize any government imposed on China by force. This of course angered Japan very much. The United States also placed an embargo on sending oil and other items that Japan desperately needed for their daily lives and war efforts. This further infuriated the Japanese government. The United States also announced a $100 million loan to the Chinese through the Export and Import Bank. It was two days after this that the Japanese joined Germany and Italy in a tri party agreement, making clear its anger at the United States.

This also meant that if the United States entered the war, they would have to conduct a war on two fronts—in Europe and Asia. The admirals and generals in Japan did not believe the United States would go to war against Japan, as they did not think the US could fight a war on two fronts.

So, on December 7, 1941, the Japanese attacked the Pearl Harbor naval base in Hawaii. Leading up to the attack, United States Navy code breakers had cracked many of the Japanese communications codes, and so they knew that the Japanese were planning an attack, but they did not know where it would be. Roosevelt still hoped that negotiations could stop it. A message was sent from Washington to the army and navy commanders in Hawaii and the Philippines, warning them of possible attacks, but the messages came too late.

At around 7:30 a.m. on Sunday, December 7, 1941, about 150 Japanese war planes rained bombs and torpedoes on many war ships in the US Pacific Fleet. The raid lasted about two hours and left Pearl Harbor in wreckage. Roughly 2,300 soldiers and marines were killed. Approximately seventy civilians were also killed, and a thousand other individuals were wounded. Nineteen

US ships, including eight battleships, were sunk or heavily damaged. Some 150 airplanes were also damaged. As terrible as the attack was, it did not damage a good part of the US Pacific Fleet's aircraft carriers because the portion of the fleet that included aircraft carriers were out at sea. Thus, they escaped destruction and were then able to be mobilized as the campaign developed. The following morning, President Roosevelt addressed both houses: "Yesterday, December 7, 1941—a date that will live in infamy—the United States of America was suddenly and deliberately attacked by naval and air forces of the Empire of Japan." At the end of the speech, he called on Congress to declare war, which it did within a few minutes.

The military experts in the United States decided that first they would defeat Hitler before they would turn their attention to Japan. American armies first fought successfully in North Africa, Sicily and Italy, moving from Rome into southern Europe. While this was taking place, plans were being developed to land British and American troops on the beaches of Normandy to enter Europe through France as well.

———

Back in New York, I worked with the Red Cross and with every organization at the college that was trying to help with the war effort. When the United States entered the war in 1941, every girl at Hunter was given an assignment in case New York City was bombed. Everyone at the school was involved in some way. On Friday afternoons, we would hold a dance with the USO for the soldiers who hadn't gone overseas yet. Since I couldn't dance, I was in charge of making sandwiches.

At home, my father and I were "air raid wardens," which meant that every night from 8 p.m. to 10 p.m. we walked up and down DeKalb Avenue, the street in front of my house, to make certain that every window in the building was blacked out in case there was an air raid over the city. Absolutely everyone was involved in the war effort. Even, my brother David, who was only nine years old at the time did his part. He and his buddies were given tin cans at DeWitt Clinton High School. Their job was to spend the week going up and down different apartment houses to collect rubber of any kind in one can, scrap iron of any kind in another, and if their cans were filled by the end of the week, they were given a free ticket to the movies. My brother took this very seriously. My mother, too, of course, was involved. She worked in the butcher's shop on Jerome Avenue checking ration coupons. I cannot stress too much how the entire nation was behind the war effort and how everyone tried to help. My family was just one example.

Working for the War Effort at Hunter College.

That was the home front, but thousands of miles away in Europe, my husband-to-be, Leonard, was experiencing the war firsthand as a GI. We didn't know each other yet, but his experiences during the war would mark him for the rest of his life and had an impact on our marriage, as well.

Leonard would rarely talk about the war. Once, when we went to the movies to see *The Longest Day*, one of the best films about the war, he started to shake so violently the usher had to help me get him into a car. With all my trips for the American Jewish Congress and later for NYU, he would never go to Europe. Only on the fiftieth anniversary of D-Day did he join some of the men at NYU who had also participated in that historic invasion to travel to Normandy for the fiftieth anniversary celebration. Everyone who fights in a war pays a very heavy price, as did every young man who was in the D-Day invasion, or any part of that war. I lived with someone who paid that price—and it clearly affected our life.

One quiet evening at our second home in Westport, we had watched another movie about the war, and I asked him whether the movie captured what the war was all about and how the soldiers felt.

"No," he said, ". . . they never can capture how much we hated the war and how scared we were in any battle we had to fight." He added that most of the men had never seen guns and certainly had never used one.

I asked him if he was involved in a lot of fighting.

"Not in the beginning," he said. "I was lucky. My first year I spent in Iceland where the United States was building an airfield for its airplanes that were going to be involved in that part of Europe. After about a year there we were sent to England for training for the Normandy invasion. On the way from Iceland to England, we had some fighting but not much. We loved our stay in England. The British nurses were very friendly and helpful. We made friends. We had very good living quarters, and it was my best time in the army, if I ever had a best time. After being trained for almost a year, my battalion landed on Normandy on the third day after the initial invasion. The beach was littered with bodies that were killed in the first and second invasion efforts—killed by the German bunkers located on the cliffs above the beaches. It was a horrible, horrible sight to see. We then joined the march with Eisenhower to Berlin."

He was referring to the fact that in the spring of '45, the Allies crossed the Rhine River from the west and advanced deep into Germany, while, in the east, the Soviets surrounded and captured Berlin. He said it was a relatively peaceful march until they got to an area that had been called the Bulge between France and Germany. The Germans made a last effort to defeat the Allies at that point in the war. They lost that effort. Leonard was injured in the Bulge and was taken by jeep to a hospital in Paris. He had three operations in the area around his vocal cords. His throat always hurt him when he spoke.

Leonard was in the hospital in Paris recovering from his injury in the Bulge in May 1945.

He did not have clear memories of his time in the hospital, but he did remember when he and the others in the hospital heard that the Germans had surrendered. He said he could not find the words to describe the happiness they felt.

He told me, "The nurses and doctors helped us get out of our beds and took us to the lawn. We kissed, we hugged, we sang, we celebrated in an ecstasy of happiness and joy. We even started to sing 'Over There.'

We all carried on until the nurses put us back to bed, but we couldn't sleep. We were so happy. After a week or so I was given additional good news. I was told that in about two more weeks, I would be sent home. I could not believe it, but I had in front of me a paper that told me so. Three weeks later, I still had bandages around my neck, but I was put on a boat back to the States. There must have been hundreds of soldiers on that boat. I was lucky to be in the infirmary section where I had a bed, bathroom, and access to a shower—something I had sorely missed. Finally, after about four days we came into New York Harbor." Then Leonard stopped and his lips started to tremble. "I know," he said, "it sounds over-emotional, but you cannot imagine how we felt when we saw the Statue of Liberty."

The men cried, they laughed, they prayed, and again they hugged each other and started to sing "The Star-Spangled Banner." Most of them, including Leonard, never thought that they would see America again.

"When I got off the boat my mother, brother, father, sister, and brother-in-law were there to greet me. I'm not sure they recognized me, as I had not shaved for several weeks, and my hair had grown long. But I recognized them, and when I got to them my mother, of course, started to cry. 'Oh, my dear,' she said, 'I sent a boy of nineteen into the war, and a man of twenty-three with a beard and long hair has come home.'"

Leonard stayed with his parents for about a month and went to the VA for treatment every few days. Soon, he was soon out on his own.

Another time I asked Leonard about the war, "Did you make any friends?"

"No, I never did," he said. "The men were very different than I was. While they never said or did anything specifically anti-Semitic, most of them had never met a Jew, and I could feel in the atmosphere a sense of anti-Semitism although it was never clearly defined. The men drank a lot whenever they could get any alcohol. They played dice and poker. I never played. They often told very dirty jokes. I never told jokes like that. In fact, I was embarrassed just to listen to them. And, I never saw them read anything, either a newspaper or a book. On the other hand, they were very brave and helpful. When I was shot, I remember them picking me up and carrying me to a jeep, even though they were under fire."

Only once did Leonard tell me about his experience seeing the concentration camps. He and his battalion landed in Normandy on the third day after the initial invasion. They marched with Eisenhower to Berlin. On the way, Eisenhower insisted that they go into every concentration camp that they passed. The soldiers were horrified at what they saw as they marched from camp to camp. Nothing that was ever shown on television in the decades to come, Leonard said, equaled the horror of what they saw in each camp. Many young soldiers came out and vomited. They pleaded with Eisenhower not to send them into the camps. He refused.

Eisenhower said, "You have to see this, so you know what you are fighting against and what you are fighting for."

What they saw was the result of the most vicious and horrible form of anti-Semitism, a scourge I have spent my whole life trying to understand. It killed six million Jews and left thousands more psychologically damaged for the rest of their lives. A great deal of my work has been dedicated to seeking to ensure that a tragedy like this never again will occur, not to the Jewish people, and not to anyone.

While Leonard was, unbeknownst to me, defending the world from fascism in Europe, back in America, I finished college and took the exam to be a history teacher in New York City public schools. I passed the written section, but I failed the oral part of the test because I had, what I was told was, "a Bronx twang." To this day I don't know what a Bronx twang is, but apparently because of it I could not teach history in New York City's public schools. I was heartsick. One of my college professors, who saw how upset I was, was able to get me a scholarship to Columbia Law School. Ultimately, I have to thank the Bronx for that twang—it led me down the path that changed my life.

Just like my time at Hunter, my three years at law school were terrific. I became an editor of the *Columbia Law Review*. Again,

I made a few new friends; and I loved the study of law. I not only loved it, but I did very well.

However, from the pictures that appear in this book, it's clear that I was not a very attractive teenage girl. I never had any boyfriends in high school, college, or at law school. So, one day three girls from law school came to me and said they were going to a doctor in Brooklyn who had a very good reputation to have their noses fixed and to have other cosmetic surgery. If I joined them, they would be able to get a discount. I not only wanted to be part of that group of girls, I also thought if I looked better I would have more friends, both boys and girls.

I spoke to my mother, who spoke to my aunts. They thought anything that would help me look better, find a man, and get married was worth the cost of the operation. The total cost for my operation would be $300. My Aunt Sadie contributed $100, my Aunt Flo $100, and my mother $100. Thus, I was able to join the group of girls who went to Brooklyn for the discounted procedure.

My mother travelled with me to Brooklyn. After the surgery we went back to the Bronx on the subway. We could not afford to take a taxi. In a few days, the cotton came out of my nose, and my new nose was revealed. The doctor did a good job. Everyone thought I looked terrific.

But my new nose was hardly my only victory in law school. One night when I was working in the library, I came upon a pamphlet on "Sutton's Hospital Case." That case in 1612 in Great Britain developed the idea of corporate fiction. Have you ever thought about how we got to the point where a corporation is treated like a person? How it can be sued and taxed like a person? That's called corporate fiction, the fiction of a corporation being treated like a person. This practice developed in England in 1612. I was fascinated with the pamphlet, and I read the entire thing, including the footnotes, instead of doing my job that night.

At Columbia Law School, there was a professor called Professor Goebel, who was a very tough teacher, and all the students were scared to death of him. He would call you up and cross examine you on topics related to the development of legal institutions. I was told there were people who almost fainted when called up to be subjected to his cross examination. Well, one day I got called up and the subject was, to my delight, the development of corporate fiction. He was shocked by all I knew and how I was able to discuss it at great length. He was so impressed that he sent a memo to the faculty telling them how brilliant I was and recommending me for the *Law Review* at the end of my first year. Professor Goebel and I soon became friends. He even came to my wedding, and we continued to have a warm friendship for many years. My classmates asked how I could be friends with that monster, but I explained he was very nice to me. That was a pure accident. Blame it on the "Sutton's Hospital Case." I am probably the only person in the United States who knows about that case.

—

It was during this exciting and stimulating period of my life that I met Leonard, who had recently returned from fighting in Europe. The war had just concluded, and there was a heady spirit of optimism throughout the city and the nation. One night, Leonard met a friend of his from college, a man who now was attending Columbia Law School. The friend invited him to a dinner he was hosting for two friends who were getting married. One of those friends was Ann, a friend of mine and one of the few women in my class at Columbia Law School. Because Ann and I were friends, I was also at this dinner.

Leonard and I liked each other from the start. He was a quiet young man. He was attending NYU for his bachelor's and master's degrees in accounting and business management, under the GI Bill. He was the opposite of my father, clearly very serious about education and work. After school every evening, he would work a few hours at his father's factory in the East Bronx. It was a small factory that made steel wool. He also worked there on Saturday and Sunday.

Whenever he wasn't studying, he was working. Since I had lived with a father who was not that serious about school and work, I found it very impressive for a young man to be so devoted to his job and to his education. We started to go out seriously and, in less than a year, we announced our engagement. We were married on April 11, 1948.

The month before my marriage, I caused havoc in my home and in Leonard's. I announced to my parents that because I did not believe in God, I did not want to be married by a rabbi. I thought my mother would have a heart attack and surely Leonard's parents, who were Orthodox Jews, were very close to a heart attack.

"How could you say that?" my mother asked, "Every Jewish person is married by a rabbi. If not, your marriage is not recognized."

One day, while they were all arguing, I took myself on the subway to 88th Street and Park Avenue, to the Park Avenue Synagogue. I walked in with no appointment. The secretary at the door, a serious gatekeeper, said that because I had no appointment and was not even a member, I could not just walk in and expect to see Rabbi Milton Steinberg. I pleaded with her, explaining that I had come to the synagogue all the way from the Bronx, and it was very critical that I see the rabbi. Apparently, Rabbi Steinberg heard us arguing and came out of his office.

"What's the problem?" he asked.

"If I have to be married by a rabbi, it has to be you and I want to explain," I said.

He took me into his office, and we had a very long discussion. I had just finished reading his book, *As a Driven Leaf.* I said it had very much impressed me, and I would deeply appreciate it if he would officiate my wedding. When I think back on this, it was really great "chutzpah" on my part to expect one of the most important rabbis in New York, who had one of the most elegant synagogues in New York City, to marry a poor girl from the Bronx, just because I (who was I after all?) liked his book.

But, after our discussion, Rabbi Steinberg said, "It would be my pleasure to marry you."

I then asked him what it would cost me.

"Whatever you can afford," he said.

"I think I can afford $100," I said.

He said that would be fine and that I could pay it over time. And so, I was married in the Park Avenue Synagogue, one of the most beautiful in New York City by one of the most important rabbis. I think my friends and family were duly impressed. And most importantly, I was impressed with how gracious, understanding, and kind Milton Steinberg was to me. We became friends and, over the years, would meet at the Madison Deli just to talk. I learned so much from him. He was a remarkable man. Unfortunately, he died very young.

*Leonard and I on our wedding day at the Park Avenue
Synagogue, after I, a poor girl from the Bronx, talked
the eminent rabbi into officiating our wedding.*

While Leonard and I settled into married life, I tried to figure out how to practice the law in a way that was fulfilling to me. Because I had been an editor of the *Law Review*, Columbia helped me get a job as soon as I graduated. They secured me a position at a big law firm. I worked there for two years, but I really did not like the work and the atmosphere of a big firm. I was assigned to trusts and estates. I found it very boring.

Holding baby Joan.

The one advantage to working at a law firm with many lawyers was that let me leave work at 5:30 p.m. One year after Leonard and I were married, we had a daughter, Joan, and leaving exactly at 5:30 meant I was able to get to Riverdale, where we lived at the time, by 6 p.m., feed Joan, bathe her, and put her to bed. We had a wonderful nanny who not only cared for Joan during the day but did all kinds of chores around the house.

Leonard playing with Joan.

During that period, Leonard and I benefited greatly from the GI Bill, which was one of the most important bills that the Congress of the United States ever enacted. The GI Bill paid for the education of soldiers after the war, if they wanted to go to college or get a graduate degree. Leonard was a student at City College before the war. After the war, he enrolled at New York University, which at that time had a superb business school (and, of course, still does today). There, he got his BA and master's degrees in business from NYU—all paid for by the government under the GI Bill. As a result of that bill, in 1946, half of the students in college were veterans and, because of that, the country had a far more educated population.

Second, because of the GI Bill, Leonard and I were able to buy a house in Hastings, New York—a suburb of Westchester County. We were newlyweds with a young child, and we did not have much money. The GI Bill allowed us to buy a house in Westchester with a very small down payment and a thirty-year mortgage that had a long-term payment schedule at very little interest. Because of this provision in the GI Bill, a great many veterans left the cities to live further from their workplace, as we did. This played a big role in the development of suburbia, but, unfortunately, left the cities to the poor, mostly to Black people who could not afford to buy a house even with the help of the GI Bill. This helped in creating the segregated housing patterns that plague us to this day.

So, thanks to the GI Bill, we had a more comfortable life than we would have had otherwise, but I still wanted and needed to work, and, the fact was, I was miserable at the big firm. On my own, I found a job with a single practitioner, Charlie Gottlieb. He took cases in every area of the law, and he only had two people working for him, Harold Schiff and me. We handled every aspect of the law from divorce to breach of contract. But again, I found that after several years with Mr. Gottlieb, I really did not like the commercial practice of law.

One evening, by chance, I attended a lecture by the director of the American Jewish Congress's Commission on Law and Social Action (CLSA). He told the audience that the American Jewish Congress believed that if any country treated the Black community the way the South treated Black people under the Jim Crow laws, the Jews would be next. Therefore, the American Jewish Congress created a Commission on Law and Social Action within the Congress that was going to devote itself to a major national program that would try and eliminate the Jim Crow Laws. I was intrigued, and I applied for a job with the commission. Phil Baum, who later became a very dear friend of mine, also applied. He got the job, not me. Will Maslow, who was general counsel to the AJC and later the executive director, in his "sensitive way" told me that Phil got the job "because he was smarter." (I learned later on that this was absolutely true). A few months later, the AJC was expanding their legal staff and added another lawyer. It was then that they hired me. I was paid $3,500 a year—it was a significant step down in my salary—but it was the job that made me who I am.

chapter three

AJC Beginnings, or an Unlucky Elevator Ride Turns Lucky

So, the dawn of the 1950s found me in a new job, finally using the law to ends I believed in: building a more perfect union. In addition to the boss, Will Maslow, Phil Baum, who had gotten the first job I had applied for, and me, the AJC had three other lawyers: Leo Pfiffer, whose books on church-state separation are still used extensively in classes on this area of juris prudence; Joe Robinson, who wrote most of the anti-discrimination laws for New York State; and Lois Waldman, who edited all the briefs that we wrote. It was an extraordinary bunch, and I am proud to say that many of the cases that went to the Supreme Court attacking the Jim Crow laws were informed by briefs written by the CLSA staff, including me. Specifically, Phil Baum and I wrote the brief in the *Sweatt v. Painter* (1950), the first case in which the Supreme Court declared the Jim Crow laws of Texas unconstitutional. We also played an important role in *Brown v. Board of Education of*

Topeka (1954), the case that eliminated segregation in the public schools of the south. The Supreme Court even quoted part of our brief in their decision.

At the same time as I was writing briefs, I also wrote many articles on school segregation and other topics relating to civil rights for the AJC's bi-weekly bulletin. These included: "From Color Blind to Color Conscious" in March 1957, "Attacking Segregation in the North" in January 1959, "Lesson of the Swastika Smearing" in December 1961, and later, "The Failure of the Community: Action Phase of the Poverty Program" in December 1969, "School Integration: Time for Reaffirmation" in April 1970, "Quotas and Affirmative Action" in November 1972, and "Affirmative Action or Equal Opportunity" in November 1973, to mention a few.

———

After about two years as a lawyer in CLSA, I became an administrator, but like everything else in my life, again, it was an accident. Here's how it happened. One day, the entire staff went out for lunch to celebrate someone's birthday. While we were out, Shad Polier, one of the members of our executive board and a difficult man, called and no one was in the office to take his call. He became very angry and spoke harshly about this to Will Maslow. Will called us together and said we could not let this happen again.

He turned to me and said, "You bring your lunch every day and eat at your desk. I think you should answer the phone so that the office is covered."

I was a very strong feminist, and I said, "I don't agree. I think we should take turns answering the phone. It should not be my responsibility only."

He was very angry with my response.

He said, "I make the rules and I believe since you eat at your desk anyway that it should be your responsibility, and if you don't like it you can quit!"

I packed up my belongings, quit, and walked out.

Actually, I was heartsick while I was doing this. I loved my job. Not only that, I needed the money and leaving something I loved hurt me very much. I got in the elevator and cried. As the elevator opened on the fourth floor, a young woman got in, saw me crying, and asked what was wrong. I told her what had happened.

"It's lucky I met you," she said. "I am going to be married this weekend. I am taking off from my job for two weeks for my wedding and honeymoon."

I learned later that her name was Carol Coan. She was marrying Dr. David Petegorsky, the executive director of the AJC.

Carole continued: "Judge Justine Wise Polier, the president of the women's division, is very unhappy because the women are having their major convention that they hold every two years while I am away. They need me, and there's a lot of work that has to be done, and there will be no one in the office to do it. Maybe you can go and help them while I am away."

So, instead of exiting the elevator in the lobby, I pressed the button for fourth floor and rode right back up to the women's division. Justine Wise Polier was delighted to have me, and from the start we got along beautifully. She was an extraordinarily impressive women, the first women judge to be appointed in the state of New York (she was also, by coincidence, married to Shad Polier, the member of the executive board who had called the legal department and found no one there to speak to him . . . the reason I was temping for her in the first place). Justine Wise Polier was the daughter of Stephen Samuel Polier, a reform rabbi and a Zionist. He was also a founding member of the NAACP.

Then when Carol came back at the end of two weeks, Justine said to her, "No, I've hired Naomi Levine in your place."

Carol was shocked, and all the assistants and interns who adored her were equally shocked and upset. But Justine Wise Polier was tough, and no one ever disagreed with any decision she made, and no one, including me, ever argued with her. For many years, there were people who thought I was a horrible person because I became the assistant director of the women's division due to Carol's firing. I have often thought about it, and I don't think that I could have behaved differently. If I said "no" to Justine, she would have fired me and hired someone else. I should add that one of the secretaries was particularly angry about what had happened and came to me to say she was going to quit because of my actions. I pleaded with her to stay on for a few weeks while I hired a substitute. This lady was Rae Weiss who stayed with me for fifty years: twenty-five at American Jewish Congress and twenty-five at NYU. There is much more to say about Rae, but all that comes later. For now, suffice it to say, that she was an indispensable part of my career and my life.

As time went on, Justine Wise Polier and I became very close both professionally and personally. Two years after my becoming the director of the women's division, Irene Arnold, asked for special time off. Judge Polier fired her and made me the director of the women's division. Without question, Justine Wise Polier made my career and taught me everything I needed to know as an executive director. My whole trajectory would have been very different without her. I doubt I would have gone into administration, and I probably would have stayed in the practice of law.

The American Jewish Congress was a very important organization in those years. It had about 100,000 members in fifteen or more chapters throughout the country. It had chapters in Manhattan, Brooklyn, Queens, and the Bronx, throughout New Jersey, and in Washington DC, Miami, Chicago, Cleveland, Detroit, San Francisco, Los Angeles, and a very important chapter in Philadelphia.

The Women's Division was the most active component of the American Jewish Congress. As the civil rights movement gained steam, the women marched, sat in, joined the bus boycott, and visited with political leaders on the state and federal level. They had meetings every month, including discussions on education and programs on activism. They were the face of the AJC in their communities. They were at the forefront of the fight for civil rights, human rights, and women's rights, and they stood in support of the state of Israel. I tried to visit every chapter of the Women's Division in the course of each year, which meant I was constantly traveling.

For my trips, I had a special format that I always followed. I would take the train (I hated flying) and arrive at my destination about 11:00 a.m. The leadership of the chapter usually met me at the train. They would help me check into a hotel, and then we spent an hour or two just talking or "schmoozing." They were wonderful women—smart, active in politics, and usually with a great sense of humor.

At noon, the chapter would hold a meeting at which I would speak. They always thought my speech was "wonderful," and I, in turn, thoroughly enjoyed these trips, the women I met, and, most of all, their accolades. I was vain enough to savor every complimentary word and all the applause they gave me. In the evening, they usually arranged a dinner in my honor together with the men's division. I spoke again at the dinner and, again, the applause and accolades I received after the evening meeting continued to feed my ego and vanity.

The next day, I would usually meet with the local federation and/or the Large City Budgeting Committee (LCBC) and a radio station or newspaper for an interview. I returned home late that afternoon, still carrying with me all the praise I usually received. There is something special about bonding between women, and, in this period, I developed warm relationships with the AJC's remarkable women's leadership throughout the country.

chapter four

Camp Greylock

———★———

The mid-'50s were a turning point in my life. Hastings, where we lived, was very beautiful, but Leonard and I hated it there. It wasn't for us, and we disliked commuting very much. So, as I mentioned, we moved to 415 West End Avenue, and then, we moved to 451 West End Avenue, to an apartment that was just like Aileen's, and we stayed in Manhattan the rest of our lives.

Still, when Justine Wise Polier came to me and said that she and Shad were going to Europe for a month during the summer and then asked if I would I like to housesit while she was away, I was delighted. She had a very beautiful house in Nyack, New York, in a community that had many houses facing the Hudson River. Even though I had loved being back in the city, I jumped at the offer. The house was big enough for my mother and father to stay with me. During the week, Leonard worked in New York and came up only for the weekends. Staying in Nyack in the summer was also a relief for me as a mother. This was just before the polio vaccine was invented. Being out of New York City meant that Joan was isolated from the virus, and I was less anxious.

One day, Sam Brown, who was the field director for New Jersey for the AJC, told me that he and a friend were looking to buy a summer camp and asked if Leonard and I would like to drive with them on some Saturday or Sunday to accompany them. He always respected my opinion, and he said he would appreciate my joining him. Again, I was delighted because the truth is I was getting a little bored, and this gave me an adventure for the weekend. Over the next month, we visited at least seven camps.

I had never gone to camp or worked at one, but I still had the nerve to comment after each visit, making sure that Sam heard me say, "If I were doing it, I would do it differently."

Both Sam and Leonard thought I had a lot of "chutzpah" to say this, since I was so ignorant about camping.

That winter, though we got a call from Mr. Berg, one of the real estate people who had taken us out months before. He had a camp in the Adirondacks called Camp Greylock. The lady who ran it and made it a very successful camp had died, and her children had run it into the ground. They were close to bankruptcy. Mr. Berg offered to take Leonard and me up to the Adirondacks, put us up in a motel, and show us the area and the camp.

I said to Leonard, "We have nothing to lose. We have never been in the Adirondacks, and here we have a chance to see a whole new part of New York and someone else is paying for it."

So, we went up to the Adirondacks, a six-hour drive from New York City. This was before the construction of the New York State Thruway.

An aerial photo of Camp Greylock.

The camp was in a very remote area of the Adirondacks on Raquette Lake, the fourth largest lake in New York State with a ninety-eight-mile shoreline. When we got to the camp, I was mesmerized by how beautiful the area was. Raquette Lake was covered with ice, and the trees surrounding the lake had icicles hanging from their branches. The lake is "forever wild" under the Constitution of the State of New York, and both it and the forest that met us were so beautiful I cannot find the words to express it. If a person can fall in love with a physical place, I fell in love with Camp Greylock at that moment.

When we got back to New York City, I found out that the hundred acres on Raquette Lake could be bought for $125,000, inclusive of all the camp equipment on the premises. I was very eager to move forward, but Leonard reminded me about a simple fact: we had no money. I was thirty-two years of age, Leonard was thirty-five, we had a young daughter. How could I ever think of buying a camp with no money and no experience?

But, for reasons that I will never know, I was determined to have this camp. I had a very good job at AJC, and I certainly didn't need another area of employment at this point in my life. Since I had no money, Leonard assumed that the issue was closed. Even though he and I were married a few years, he really didn't know me. When I get a thought in my head, it's very hard to get it out. I wanted that camp. I asked him to go back and try and negotiate a lower bid. He was furious, but, at that point in our relationship, he loved me enough to do what I really wanted. He said he would go back and make an offer of $65,000.

"Are you crazy?" I said to him. "That's an embarrassing amount for a hundred acres and a camp. I'm not going."

He said that he would go alone, and, somehow, on that trip, he convinced them to take the $65,000. How he did that, I will never know. I suspect that the camp was in such a bad economic state that the owners were willing to take anything.

We then had to go and get $65,000. I persuaded the sellers, the Mason family, to take $30,000 down; the rest I was sure I could get in a mortgage. My mother and father were staunchly opposed to this crazy idea, but they were always very loyal to me. They were poor people, so all my mother had was $2,500. Leonard's parents had $25,000. Judge Polier then took me to Chase Bank where they gave me the balance. She was the cosigner on the loan. At the time, the slogan for Chase Manhattan Bank was, "You have a friend at Chase Manhattan." I certainly did and always told disbelieving friends that Chase gave me the money because of that slogan.

So, then, I had a camp. I had no idea what to do, really, but I thought the first thing I should do was get acquainted with the physical layout. Sam Brown had given up the idea of owning a camp himself, but he knew a great deal about camping through some experiences he had had as a younger man. He accompanied Leonard and me on a tour of the grounds, and we discovered, to my dismay, that the camp needed at least $100,000 in renovations before we could open it. The kitchen was a mess, the septic system was terrible, and the state would not approve the opening of a camp with a septic system that required so much updating.

"Okay," Leonard said, "Now you got yourself in a bind. You have a camp, and you can't open it."

Again, he didn't know me. I was very good friends with a colleague from before the AJC, a young man called Howard Squadron. We grew up on the same block in the Bronx. His younger brother played basketball with my brother, and we had a very friendly relationship. Howard went to Columbia Law School and was a first year when I was a third. Howard's mother-in-law lent "schlock money," meaning money lent at tremendous interest rates. So, I went and borrowed $100,000 from Howard's mother-in-law at exorbitant interest rates. The money was used to fix up the camp and especially its septic system. In the summer of 1955, we opened a girls' camp. The only children at the camp were the children of friends of mine. They hardly paid any money, but at least it gave me an opportunity to try out with these children what I thought a camp should be.

I was my own program director. I had a philosophy about camping. I believed that a summer camp should, of course, give the girls an opportunity to learn swimming, canoeing, water skiing, sailing, tennis, and all the sports that camps traditionally provide. But I thought that it also should provide some intellectual excitement and stimulation that would add to the girls' knowledge.

I wanted all aspects of camp life to be directed towards learning—both skills and interpersonal relations. In general, I believe that the most exciting experiences of life are learning experiences. Camp, I thought, should be no exception. There is no dichotomy between learning and having fun, if the teacher is a good one, the learner properly motivated, and the atmosphere a pleasant and relaxed one. Camp, I posited, should be viewed as both an educational as well as a recreational medium. I wanted Greylock to provide a wide range of instruction in the many skills that people learn best when they are young—on the water, on the playing fields, and in the arts, music and drama. It was also important to me that Greylock provide an atmosphere in which young women could learn to live completely away from home, including how to handle interpersonal conflicts without the constant supportive aid of their parents. I wanted Greylock to provide a wide and diversified program, with enough free time for relaxation, making friends, and just thinking, daydreaming, and learning to live in a peer group.

IMPORTANT INSTRUCTIONS

Saks Fifth Avenue's CAMPERS SHOP has been appointed our Official Outfitter. In the Campers Shop you will find a specially-trained staff to assist you in making your selections. Fine quality, good-looking camping clothes and equipment are available at sensible prices. The Campers Shop will open about the second week in March and remain open through June.

YOU MAY ORDER BY 'PHONE. Call

PLaza 3-4000, ask for the Campers Shop

YOU MAY ORDER BY MAIL. Write

Campers Shop
Saks Fifth Avenue
611 Fifth Avenue
New York 22, New York

IMPORTANT: When ordering by mail

1. Fill in number of items needed in boxes provided on right hand column
2. Fill in measurement chart completely
3. Return the entire outfitting list

This will supply all the information necessary for the prompt and accurate filling of your order.

Saks Fifth Avenue WILL FURNISH PRICES upon request

MEASUREMENT CHART

Age.......... Height.......... Weight..........

Slender □   Average □   Chubby □

Clothing Size ....

Shoe Size .... Hose Size ....

Head Size ....

Bust Measurement .... Waist Measurement ....

Hip Measurement (at widest part)...........

Outseam Measurement (from waist to ankle) ....

Camp Name ....

Camper's Name ....

Parent's Name ....

Address ....

Charge □   Check or Money Order □

I Wish To Open a Saks Fifth Avenue Charge Account.
Please Send Me an Application Blank □

CAMP GREYLOCK
ON
RAQUETTE LAKE
Raquette Lake, New York

Directors:

NAOMI LEVINE
LEONARD LEVINE

New York Office:
451 West End Avenue
New York 24, New York
TRafalgar 3-5084

Official Outfitter:

SAKS FIFTH AVENUE
At Rockefeller Center
White Plains N.Y.   Springfield N.J.
Garden City N.Y.

Camp Greylock pamphlet front and back.

GIRLS' OFFICIAL UNIFORM

AVAILABLE FROM SAKS FIFTH AVENUE

The Camp Colors are Green and Brown

(on hand / needed)

6 White Blouses
6 White Fashion Collar Shirts with Greylock Painted Design
4 Pairs Dark Green Cotton Shorts
2 Pairs Brown Cotton Shorts
1 Pair Dark Green Cotton Bermuda Shorts
2 Pairs Dark Green Slacks
5 Pairs Dungarees, Cut (Knee Length)
1 Dark Green Blazer with Emblem
1 Dark Blue Sweat Shirt
1 Sailing Parka, any color (Seniors only)
1 Dark Green Sweater, V-Neck
20 Pairs Socks (White, Brown, Green)
1 Navy Blue One Piece Swim Suit

SPECIAL INSTRUCTIONS

1. NAME TAPES SHOULD BE SEWED AS FOLLOWS:
A. In neckband of shirts, pajama tops, underwear.
B. Inside center back of waistline of pajamas, shorts, underwear.
C. On outside corner of sheets.
D. On outside of hem of pillow cases and towels.
E. On inside top of each sock.
2. All articles including traveling clothes must be marked with full name of camper.
3. Please put loops for hanging, on wash cloths, towels, bathrobes. On towels, loops to be in center of long side.
4. Please pack socks in a small box that can be used in bureau drawer all summer.
5. Please do not use tray trunks.
6. EXTRA NAME TAPES SHOULD BE BROUGHT TO CAMP.

NAME TAPES MAY BE PURCHASED AT SAKS FIFTH AVENUE WHERE THEY WILL BE SEWN ON AT NO ADDITIONAL CHARGE.

NECESSARY ARTICLES

Bedding and Linen

(on hand / needed)

3 Heavy Green Blankets with Emblem
6 Sheets (54 x 99)
8 Pillow Cases
8 Bath Towels
4 Wash Cloths
1 Rubber Sheet and Extra Bed Sheets (if necessary)
1 Laundry Bag

Toilet Articles

Soap, Comb, Hair Brush, Mirror, Toothbrush, Toothpaste, Nail Brush, File, Barrettes, Bobby Pins, Scissors, Kleenex.

Footwear

(on hand / needed)

1 Pair Sneakers (Smooth Soles)
1 Pair Moccasin Oxfords
1 Extra Pair Shoes
1 Pair Bedroom Slippers
1 Pair Bathing Shoes
Galoshes or Rubbers
1 Shoe Bag

Clothing

(on hand / needed)

1 Heavy Jacket
Several Heavy Sweaters
1 Hooded Sweatshirt
1 Cotton Flannel Shirt (Plain or Plaid)
Several Pairs Warm Slacks
Several Pairs Blue Jeans
4 Pairs Pajamas (2 Warm)
1 Bathrobe or Terry Robe
1 Bathing Suits
1 White Bathing Cap
8 Undershirts

(Clothing — continued)

(on hand / needed)

Raincoat and Hat
14 Pairs Underpants

Miscellaneous

(on hand / needed)

Camp Trunk
Duffel Bag and Lock
1 Poncho or Sleeping Bag and Blanket Pins
Flashlight and Batteries
Tennis Racquet and Balls
Extra Pair of Eyeglasses, if Camper Wears Glasses
60 Postcards and Envelopes Addressed to Parents of Younger Children

SUGGESTED ARTICLES

Fountain Pen   Musical Instruments
Books and Games   Camera and Films
Any Color Shirts, Sweaters and Shorts for Free Night

OFFICIAL OUTFITTERS:

In New York City and Vicinity:

Saks Fifth Avenue   Rockefeller Center, N. Y.
                      White Plains, N. Y.
                      Springfield, N. J.
                      Garden City, L. I.

In Pennsylvania:

Gimbels   Philadelphia, Pa.
                      Cheltenham, Pa.
                      Upper Darby, Pa.

Camp Greylock pamphlet interior.

So, I hired Helen Horowitz (the wife of my brother David), a cultural anthropologist, and in June we sent the girls three books about contemporary issues that I wanted them to read before camp opened. Obviously, the reading program was only for children aged eleven to sixteen. We read books on rainy days or in the evenings, and we spent a lot of time talking about women's role in society. I thought if I could teach them one thing, it was this, that it was important for them to know that they could do anything they wanted, and they could do it as well as or better than their male colleagues. Their mothers, by the way, were very pleased with this, which surprised me. For the most part, these girls' mothers were affluent and spent most of their time at country clubs. When I would write to them summarizing what we were doing at camp, they were ecstatic. They wanted their girls to do more with their lives than they had done.

Helen would meet with the girls after taps at night in my cabin or at an appropriate time during the day and talk about women's issues. I also insisted that all the children, even the six-year-olds, read *The New York Times* on Sunday and after breakfast, lunch, and dinner, I would go through *The Times* with them, talking about some of the issues that the paper had covered. The children actually liked this. They all had opinions, and I made sure that all their opinions were expressed.

A beautiful day for sailing on Raquette Lake.

Swimming Lessons at Greylock.

At that time, I was, of course, very much involved in the struggle for integration through my work at the AJC. I had many counselors from the South, and I encouraged them to speak their piece, and they did. Our conversations were of interest to all our campers, and I think it inspired the girls to read about and seek to understand issues like integration and segregation. I wanted them to feel free to discuss their feelings on such difficult topics and to carry their knowledge and opinions with them back to their homes after the summer was over, and, indeed, throughout their lives.

As I mentioned, that first summer, we had hardly any enrollment. Our campers were mostly children of my friends who felt sorry for me. However, the second summer, I was very lucky. One of the leading women in the AJC offered to help me. It seemed to me that she knew everyone in Philadelphia. She introduced me around town, and I was apparently a good salesperson, because the next year my enrollment went up and, in a few years, I went from forty to 150 girls enrolled in Camp Greylock.

Other camp owners that I met along the way were amazed that the girls tolerated Greylock's emphasis on reading and on current events. But, the Greylock girls loved it. They loved speaking out on all sorts of issues, they loved arguing with me, and I encouraged them to do so. I never took a rigid position. I always made it clear that their opinions were as important as mine.

Joan starring in a play at Greylock.

*My nephew, Jeffrey, when he was little, watching
the raising of the American flag at Greylock.*

The head of my drama department, David Rattner, developed a magnificent program for us that was very sophisticated and required that the girls study musical theater. His wife was in charge of the French department at the High School of Music and Art, and she developed a little French curriculum with songs and poems for us at the camp. And, because of my role at the AJC, I was able to bring up to the camp many distinguished people who talked to the girls, including Howard Squadron (yes, the same man whose mother-in-law had loaned me the schlock money—he was also a very important lawyer), Betty Friedan (when *The Feminine Mystique* came out, I sent it to all the girls ages 11–16 to read in advance of camp that summer, so we could talk about it), and Rabbi Arthur Hertzberg. All of these elements added to what I viewed as the richness of the program.

Field athletics at Greylock.

Campers canoeing on Raquette Lake.

While there was emphasis at Greylock on learning, there was little or no intracamp competition. Children were not asked to compete against other children in the camp. They were only judged by their own efforts and improvements. We did, of course, have teams that swam and played against other camps, but these were composed of volunteers. Only those children who enjoyed competition volunteered. We also had a three-day color war within the camp which provided a minimum amount of competition within the camp. We did this deliberately on the theory that you cannot eliminate all competition from a child's life. The fact is, the world they will live in is highly competitive. They needed to be exposed, therefore, to some competition and have some experience in winning and losing. It is especially important that children learn how to lose graciously and to understand cooperation and good sportsmanship. These are not old fashioned, schoolbook virtues. They are essential in every aspect of living—in school, in business, and in one's personal life.

After a few years, Greylock was recognized as one of the best girls' camps in the country. I paid a big price for that honor. We never really made money because any money we made went to paying off the mortgage and heavy loans. This upset Leonard very much. He was an accountant, and he hated being leveraged to the gills. I must confess that our marriage suffered accordingly. The fact of Greylock was also difficult for Joan. She was sharing her mother with hundreds of other children, and, on weekends, instead of me being home with her and her father, I was in Philadelphia scaring up campers. Still, Greylock was a huge part of my life. I do not understand why I bought it or why I kept it for twenty years when my family, my husband, and my child disliked it. Still, it was incredibly important to me.

Though Greylock brought me much joy, this was a difficult period in other ways. Around the time that I bought the camp, I developed anxiety attacks. They may or may not have been related to the burdens of running it. If you've never had an anxiety attack, you have no idea how painful and frightening it is. During an attack, my heart would beat very rapidly, I thought I was ready to faint, I could hardly breathe, and I was in a state of acute panic. While I had the attacks, Leonard had to take me to work by taxi in the morning, and Rae Weiss, my secretary, took me home at night. Once I was at work, I was fine. I could conduct meetings, write proposals, deal with correspondence, handle the phone, and feel okay, but outside of the office, I was a mess.

At that time, my mother worked at Montefiore Hospital, and she was able to find a very good psychiatrist for me whose office was just six blocks from where I lived. Twice a week Leonard would walk me to her office—this was because, during an attack, I could not walk alone. I could do nothing alone, as I was sure I would faint. Poor Joan remembers marching with Leonard and me twice a week to the psychiatrist's office. Sessions were fifty minutes, so Leonard and Joan had to wait outside the doctor's building because by the time they walked home, they would have to turn around to pick me up. Joan has nothing but unhappy memories of those walks. I don't believe the therapy helped me, but the drugs they put me on did. I was put originally on Dexamyl and later

Valium. Luckily, after a few years the attacks disappeared, and thank goodness, they never came back.

No one was ever able to explain to me what caused those attacks and what made them go away. And while I have been fortunate to not have any anxiety attacks again in the decades since, some of their symptoms still remain with me. I can't go anywhere alone. I need someone to go with me whether I am going on a speaking engagement, going shopping, or going to a movie. It's no problem because I have had several secretaries that have gone with me to all my business meetings, and Leonard was sensitive enough to my problems to be with me socially. We went to the country together, we entertained together, we went shopping together, and I was okay in all those situations together with him. The fact that I was able to be so successful professionally with this problem hanging like a cloud over my head is a miracle. But I was able to do it, and I am grateful for it.

I ran Camp Greylock for Girls for many years. We finally closed it in 1971. In 1995, we held a reunion at Raquette Lake. Most of the Greylock girls attended. These were women in their forties, fifties, and sixties. These were women who had developed incredible careers as doctors, lawyers, entrepreneurs, writers, dramatists and more. They had families, children—incredibly rich lives. They were thrilled to be back. But the most thrilling, marvelous part of the reunion was knowing that I had a hand instilling confidence and independence into the lives of these women. It was fulfilling to learn that I had empowered these women to stand up for themselves and know that they could do anything.

chapter five

A Decade of Progress and Turmoil

A merica is the land that gave my family so many opportunities, the land that allowed us to move out of shtetl poverty
and become educated and free. But it was clear to me, as it was to
many, that our nation was not yet living up to its potential or its
promise. Through my work at the AJC, I became very involved in
the civil rights movement, and though my legal work in support
of the cause began in the 1950s, my activism really picked up in
the 1960s.

Beginning in 1954, the civil rights movement concerned itself
largely with eliminating the legal basis of discrimination through
the enactment of antidiscrimination legislation and through
court action—during that period I was completely dedicated to
this cause. But this was not enough. Legal action needed to be
backed up by public support, so civil rights leaders developed
other strategies.

A major technique of the movement involved the Freedom Riders. In 1961, civil rights leaders were looking for a more nationally visible form of protest to get the federal government involved in their struggle, and they found it in the Freedom Riders. In December 1960, the Supreme Court had ruled that segregation in interstate bus terminals was illegal, but most of the southern terminals ignored the rule. James Farmer, director of CORE (the Congress of Racial Equality) organized integrated bus trips of both blacks and whites to travel through the south. As Jim Callan writes in *America in the 1960s,*

> Part of the plan was to have blacks attempt to use the white facilities at every stop in the terminal. Farmer believed that if violence occurred the federal government would have to intervene . . . . The first trouble came in May 1961 in Anniston, Alabama, when a mob of whites smashed the windows, slashed the tires, and firebombed one bus of the freedom riders. Neither local law enforcement nor the federal government intervened. Another bus suffered a worse fate when it reached Alabama. A large group of whites led by the local KKK attacked the freedom riders with bats, pipes, and chains, injuring many of them. On May 20, there was a similar attack on a group of twenty-one freedom riders in Montgomery, Alabama, which prompted the US Attorney General Robert Kennedy to send in the United States Marshals to protect the riders.[1]

Many women (and some men) from the American Jewish Congress joined the bus riders and several were hurt. I myself was on one bus, but I was not hurt. Farmer's plan was dangerous and risky and many paid a huge price to see it through, but ultimately it succeeded. Farmer's idea was really quite brilliant. As Callan notes,

Throughout the summer of 1961, freedom riders traveled throughout the south challenging segregation. In Mississippi, local law enforcement filled jails with riders. In September, President Kennedy ordered the Interstate Commerce Commission to forbid national bus companies from using segregated terminals. The southern terminals had to integrate or go out of business. It was a small victory for the civil rights movement.[2]

A major victory for the movement, of course, the one that everyone remembers, was the March on Washington led by Martin Luther King, Jr. The AJC played a very important role in preparing for that march, and, indeed, I was lucky enough to help organize it. Here is how that came about: Bayard Rustin was a close friend and colleague of Martin Luther King, Jr. He was the man who did all the "behind the scenes" work in organizing the march. We at the AJC provided Rustin a room in our building in which to work and also offered him secretarial help. (The AJC had a beautiful five story mansion at 15 East 84th Street between 5th Avenue and Madison Avenue, given to us by a dedicated donor.) In exchange for helping organize the march, we asked that our president, Rabbi Joachim Prinz, be allowed to march next to King and have a role as a speaker. He agreed.

Rabbi Prinz had been one of the most distinguished rabbis in Berlin and escaped to the United States before Hitler destroyed the synagogues of Berlin. My colleague Phil Baum, who at that time had been promoted to the role of director of international affairs at the AJC, and I worked on writing Rabbi Prinz's speech, the one that Prinz would give during the March on Washington. Phil was a magnificent writer. I helped him. We named the speech "The Issue is Silence." I don't recall exactly where the title came from, but it expressed beautifully what Rabbi Prinz wanted to say. He bemoaned the fact that while Hitler was gaining support, the Jews in Germany remained relatively silent. He felt that most of the Jewish community viewed Hitler as some kind of nut and thought he would disappear from the scene. The speech also told the story of how the German people watched on as the Jews suffered—and, for the most part, said nothing. They, too, were silent. Prinz wanted to make sure that in America we learned that lesson, that silence in the face of injustice is a sin.

We thought our speech was wonderful, and Rabbi Prinz liked it, too. He did indeed march next to King and deliver his speech, but after King's magnificent "I Have A Dream," nobody cared one iota about our speech on silence. But Rabbi Prinz did take the talk on his many speaking tours and continued to use it as the basis of many speeches he made throughout the United States, so our effort was not a total waste of our time.

In general, the '60s were a time of great turbulence, and it seemed that for every victory in the name of progress, there was a great tragedy. One of my most important, most salient memories from the beginning of the 1960s is, as it was for many, a day in late November, 1963. I was walking back from a meeting when President John F. Kennedy was shot. When I arrived at 15 East 84th Street, I found the entire AJC staff in the library huddled around a radio, everyone crying. At that point, I learned that President Kennedy had been assassinated. I could hardly believe it. I joined the crying, too.

Kennedy was the symbol of a new youthful world—a Camelot. He had great ideas for a "new frontier" for this country. He wanted every citizen to have good healthcare, a first-rate education, a job, and enough money to have decent housing. He had a tremendous ability to move people and inspire them through his speeches. I remember attending one of his rallies in New York City. He was a war hero, saving his crew on the patrol torpedo boat PT-109 after it was wrecked by a Japanese torpedo on August 2, 1943. He was a president that the country trusted. He represented strength and credibility.

Kennedy was truly a great leader, though he had made mistakes as a president, of course. For example, in 1959 Fidel Castro, a Communist, overthrew the government of Fulgencio Batista, the corrupt ruler of Cuba. Castro seized foreign businesses, many owned by the United States, and became friendly with the Soviet Union, taking aid from them. Eisenhower and the administration around him were distraught. Cuba was only ninety miles from Florida. They decided to invade Cuba and assassinate Castro. When Kennedy became president, he asked the CIA to go over those plans with him and, on April 17, 1961, Kennedy approved a plan to invade Cuba via an area called the Bay of Pigs on the southern coast of the island. The goal was to assassinate Castro. Unfortunately, the plan was a disaster. Castro knew the invasion was coming. The 1,500 US-trained Cuban exiles set to invade were met by 20,000 Cuban troops and imported Soviet artillery. Apparently, the United States was going to use an assassin from the mafia, but they never had a chance. Two days later, 114 Cuban exiles and Americans were dead. Kennedy went on television to apologize to the American public for his botched attempt to kill Castro. This mission angered the Soviet Union, and it subsequently ramped up more military aid to Cuba. It was a ridiculous plan that went very bad. I was surprised that Kennedy, a smart man, would have moved in this direction. Of course, even smart people sometimes make stupid mistakes.

Still, Kennedy did not give up on trying to get rid of Fidel Castro. Throughout 1962, his military advisers and the CIA worked on various schemes that included a direct invasion of Cuba itself. Kennedy wanted Castro removed or overthrown, but he was fearful of a direct invasion as he worried that it might cause a nuclear war with the Soviet Union.

In the end, instead of a direct invasion, he authorized an embargo on Cuba. He also authorized more military exercises in the Caribbean which tested US Naval readiness in case of war with Cuba. In April of that year, he authorized the placement of nuclear weapons in Turkey near the Turkey-Soviet border.

Khrushchev was very angry about the US missiles in Turkey and the US Naval exercises in the Caribbean. The Soviet Union was sure that this indicated the United States was serious about an invasion of Cuba. Castro was very fearful of such an invasion and therefore agreed to accept that nuclear missiles from the Soviet Union be placed on Cuban territory. In July of that year, the missiles were being sent to Cuba—secretly.

During August and September, Soviet ships continued to deliver materials to Cuba to build the missile sites. The United States gathered this information from U-2 spy planes. They asked the Soviet Union frequently if the missiles were for defense or offense. The Soviets repeatedly stated that the weapons were defensive.

They were lying. In October, photos from a U-2 mission showed that the weapons were offensive nuclear missiles with a range of up to twenty-five miles. From this distance, they could attack the United States. Kennedy did not inform the American public of this for several days. In the meantime, Kennedy and his advisers agreed that the missiles in Cuba had to be removed, but this carried the risk of a nuclear war. His advisers urged an airstrike to destroy the weapons, but this also risked invoking a Soviet response that could result in a nuclear war. Kennedy decided to impose a naval blockade around Cuba, stopping further shipments of missiles and military equipment to Cuba. He went to the United Nations and showed them the U-2 photos indicating that the Soviets were placing in Cuba weapons that were capable of offensive war against the United States. He urged the UN to have the Soviet Union remove the existing missiles.

On October 22, Kennedy went on television to inform the American public of the crisis. As Jim Callan writes:

The entire nation held its breath. A poll showed that most Americans expected a nuclear war. Khrushchev gave orders for the Soviet ships to continue on course, but to everyone's surprise, when they reached the US Navy ships at the blockade line they stopped and turned back.[3]

The United Nations ambassador from the United States continued to work at the UN in trying to minimize this crisis. Finally, Khrushchev agreed to remove the nuclear missiles, but only if the United States removed its nuclear missiles from Turkey. The United States agreed to remove the missiles from Turkey but did not reveal this to the public because Kennedy did not want it to appear that the United States altered its policy as a result of a nuclear threat.

On November 2, President Kennedy announced that dismantling the nuclear sites in Cuba had begun. Everyone sighed in relief. Kennedy himself that said there were no victors, only survivors.

At the time, my brother David was deeply involved with Kennedy's foreign policy efforts, though not with Cuba specifically. David was a very special man. He was brilliant with a great sense of humor. He was nine years younger than I was, and so, in many ways, I helped my mother raise him. He was a very difficult young boy, and my mother often turned to me to be a surrogate mother for him. When David was around twelve years old, he hitchhiked to Florida . . . just because he wanted to go there. The story was in *The New York Daily News*. I was in college, and I was mortified.

David received his BA from the University of Chicago and graduated from Harvard Law School in 1956. He never wanted to work in commercial law or at a private law firm. He always wanted to work in government. He started his professional career as a clerk in the tax court. He then moved over to the World Bank and then worked for the Agency for International Development (AID) as an attorney.

Around this time, JFK announced the formation of the Alliance for Progress, which was a program to bring democratic reform to the nations of Latin America. David started working as an attorney for the Alliance and later became its director. Many of the programs that the Alliance developed in Latin America were designed by David.

I cannot write about David without mentioning his wonderful wife, Helen. In 1957, David married Helen Allentuck. She was a student at Bennington College. Her mother had asked me to introduce her to David as she was on an internship program in Boston and didn't know anyone. Her mother was the president of the Bronx division of the American Jewish Congress and since, at that time, I had just been named the new director of the women's division, I did not dare turn down her request. I pleaded with David to have a drink with Helen, and the rest is history. They had two children, Jeffrey and Elizabeth.

So, as a family and a nation, we were heartbroken when Kennedy was assassinated. Moreover, Vice President Lyndon Johnson, who took office immediately after Kennedy's death, appeared on the surface at least to be the opposite of Kennedy. He was not charming or good looking, nor did he make eloquent speeches. But he was a master politician and was determined to make Kennedy's goals a reality.

My brother David did not approve of the new administration's approach to Latin America nor did he like the individual President Johnson put in charge of The Alliance for Progress. So, David left the State Department. David and Helen found themselves in Cambridge, Massachusetts, while David taught at the Kennedy School of Government.

I cannot emphasize enough that this was a very sad moment in American history. Kennedy's death seemed to place a curtain over the prospects for tomorrow. But the country also appeared vital enough to pull itself out of this malaise and go on with strength.

My life in the 1960s was almost as hectic as the political scene. In addition to all of my work at the AJC, I also began teaching at the John Jay College of Criminal Justice, a school that specializes in the education of police officers. I felt, and so did the president of the school, that my course on the law and politics of race relations was very important for future police officers. I taught for many years there and learned as much from the officers and their attitudes on race relations as they learned from me.

Eleanor Roosevelt and I at an AJC Women's Division Event.

Because the AJC was one of the largest and most vocal Jewish organizations of its times, I had the privilege of meeting many important people, both in the United States and abroad. I met usually in groups, but sometimes alone, with Eleanor Roosevelt, President Jimmy Carter, New York Governor Nelson

Rockefeller, New York Senator Jacob Javits, New York City Mayor Ed Koch, New York Senator Robert Wagner, and scores of other political leaders, as well as the heads of other Jewish and non-Jewish organizations. When I went to Israel it usually was with a group of important Jewish leaders. We met with Golda Meir, David Ben-Gurion, Moshe Dayan, and Israeli leaders from many areas of activity, like education, medical care, child development, etc. The opportunity to meet with such exciting people and to make the friends that I did at AJC made my life there a very unusual adventure.

New York State Senator Robert Wagner
and I are in our later years.

Greeting former Prime Minister of Israel David Ben-Gurion.

After I stayed with the women's division for five years, I went on to become the director of organizations and programs for the entire American Jewish Congress. In that role, I worked on programs for every chapter in the country, helped organize new chapters, brought in new leadership, and developed programs that attracted new people. I held that job for years.

During this period, there was another happy development in my life, which was that Leonard, my brother David, and I bought a house on Fire Island. Fire Island is a very special place. Cars are prohibited throughout the island. Our house was in a community called Seaview. We were able to get to Seaview by taking a ferry from Bay Shore on Long Island. Every Friday afternoon, Will Maslow and his wife, Phil Baum and his wife, Betty and Mal Warshaw, and Leonard and I would take the ferry at Bay Shore. All of our possessions went with us on the ferry. When we arrived at Fire Island, we put everything we brought with us into a small red wagon that was provided by the island and dragged our belongings to our house.

Beginning Friday night, we played poker and then continued to play the entire weekend. We argued about every issue on the AJC agenda. We argued more than we played. Each couple brought food for one meal, so we did not have to waste time cooking. We hardly ever went to the beach.

On Sunday night, we would take the last ferry out of Seaview, get into our car at Bay Shore, and drive home. It was a true retreat from the world, even as we spent much our time discussing world affairs, which weighed heavy on our minds.

I say this because, like many others, I spent much of the 1960s dismayed by the state of the nation, which was making huge leaps forward for progress, yes, but was also marked by violent conflict.

For example, the 1964 the passing of the Civil Rights Act was the glorious culmination of social and legal efforts to enshrine equal rights for all. With that the legal basis for discrimination in the country was eliminated. But there was still more work to do. Because once the laws were on the books, they needed to be implemented. And—as with the question of integrating bus terminals—it soon became clear that it wasn't enough to just have laws that prohibited discrimination in employment, education, and housing. Now, Black people needed to get jobs that would actually help them achieve genuine equality in employment, they needed to be able actually get the necessary loans to move into white neighborhoods (and for real estate agents to sell them those homes), and their children needed a fair chance to attend integrated schools.

Suddenly, the issues became more complex—more confusing, more troubling, and more frustrating. Suddenly, the interconnectedness of poverty and civil rights became clear. Suddenly, the fight for integration moved from the arena abstract principal to the reality of implementation. Suddenly, the fight moved from Washington, from the Supreme Court and the hall of the legislature to every person's backyard. And, most of all, it suddenly became clear that it was indeed naive to imagine that hundreds of years of degradation, humiliation, and slavery could be wiped away quickly by anti-discrimination legislation and by the loud and persistent singing of "We Shall Overcome." Yes, we all believed that we would overcome but there was much to overcome and the "overcoming process" was going to be long and difficult. There were economic barriers to overcome; there were educational barriers to overcome; there were deep seated myths and prejudices that still separated whites and Blacks that had to be overcome; and, perhaps most importantly, there was poverty to overcome. This meant that in order truly enshrine those rights—not just in law, but in practice—the nation had to fight a war against poverty.

President Johnson took up this fight. He announced his intention to wage a war against poverty in his State of the Union Address at the beginning of 1964. This program was a tangible expression of the fact that the federal government, and indeed all government, was now playing an active role in creating conditions conducive to achieving social and economic equality. As someone deeply dedicated to the movement, I was delighted by this move and was unequivocally dedicated to this principle. The antipoverty program, whatever its deficiencies were, deserves historical recognition as the first Federal step in this direction. Its importance cannot be over-emphasized.

One important aspect of this program was that it was not specifically aimed at or advertised as a program to help the Black community. Instead, it was set up as a plan for the nation as a whole and a federal attack on social and economic ills—a program to help all poor people achieve self-sufficiency and self-respect. In fact, it helped many white people in addition to almost all of the nation's Black population. The intent was to provide education, job training, jobs, decent housing—in short, not only to push open doors of opportunity previously closed but to help Black people and others walk through to a better life.

The Elementary and Secondary School Act of 1965, for example, which was a central piece of Johnson's war on poverty, was not specifically seen as a civil rights program, but it did much to bring out progress. Its primary aim was to improve the quality of schools and education in poorer neighborhoods, which meant the major benefits fell on Black communities. Not only were programs like these the best way to attack the problems at hand, but they also quieted some of the latent opposition within the country to singling out Black people for special, visible assistance. Indeed, at the time, these seemed to me like the most effective way to help Black people lift themselves out of poverty and into mainstream American life.

The poverty program was also designed to keep major responsibility for fighting the war in states, cities, communities, and neighborhoods. The federal government provided the federal funds to finance the ideas to combat poverty, but the local governments had to provide the ideas. This posed a significant challenge to states and cities, and thus increased their sense of responsibility in combating poverty. It increased the role they had to play in achieving equality and providing opportunity for minorities. And thus, it ultimately increased their role in the civil rights struggle—or at least that was the idea. In New York, for example, Governor Rockefeller was derelict. He and his administration did not stimulate ideas in a timely manner and therefore lost out on funds.

Overall, unfortunately, the antipoverty program proved a disappointment to the Black community. It was characterized as an attempt to "hold back the ocean with a finger in the dike." In other words, a miniscule effort—too little, coming too late. There was irritation and frustration with its slowness and red tape and the fact that it ultimately was only able to help a small portion of the community.

These frustrations coupled with the seemingly impossible task of implementing the anti-discrimination laws and the snail's pace that characterized the efforts made to achieve equality and integration were responsible in large part for the growth of the Black Power movement. Black Power as a cry for black dignity and black self-respect was a healthy cry. Still, as time went on, it became more difficult to build a coalition between Blacks and whites around these issues and violence and dissatisfaction grew throughout the nation.

By 1968, President Johnson had enough with the general national unrest, and, in particular, the Vietnam War protests; he was not beloved, as JFK had been. After a very close New Hampshire primary, where Eugene McCarthy, an anti-war politician from Minnesota, received over 42 percent of the vote, Johnson declined to run again. To me, one of the saddest results of the Vietnam War was that it denied President Johnson the ability to move forward on his war against poverty and his dream for a great society. That dream was to make America really a great place.

Calvin Mackenzie and Robert Weisbrot do a fabulous job of defining Johnson's plan in their book, *The Liberal Hour*. They write,

> A great society, where every child can find knowledge to enrich his mind and to enlarge his talents . . . it is a place where the city of man serves not only the needs of the body and the demands of commerce but the desire for beauty and the hunger of the community. It is a place where men are more concerned with the quality of life than with the quantity of their goods. Most of all the great society is not a resting place, a final objective, a finished work. It is a challenge constantly renewed becoming for us a destiny where the meaning of our lives matches the modest product of our labor.[4]

Johnson wanted a world where people not only could live safely and where the poor were taken care of, but he wanted to build a nation where people could enjoy arts and culture and could have a good job, a good education, and good health care. He wanted a "great society," and the Vietnam war denied him that goal. It also denied him the right to be viewed as a great president.

Johnson was grateful to the Congress for all the parts of his agenda that they were able to enact, but he was worried of course about the war and the costs of the war. Some congressmen said you could not afford both a war and the great society – guns and butter. Johnson disagreed, believing we were a rich country and there is no reason we could not do both. Unfortunately, the war did keep him from achieving his goals. He later told his biographer,

> I knew from the start I was bound to be crucified either way I moved. If I left the woman I already loved— the great society—in order to get involved with that bitch of a war on the other side of the world then I would lose everything at home: all my hopes to feed the hungry and shelter the homeless, all my dreams to provide education and medical care to the Browns and the Blacks and the Lame and the Poor. But if I left that war and let the communists take over South Vietnam then I would be seen as a coward and my nation would be seen as an appeaser and we would both find it impossible to accomplish anything for anybody anywhere on the entire globe. Losing the great society was a terrible thought but not so terrible at the thought of being responsible for America's losing a war to the communists. Nothing could be worse than that.[5]

Clearly, Johnson was caught between the disastrous reality of the war and the dreams he had for the nation. As a long-time politician, it was heart-breaking for him to not run for office again in 1968. So, the Democratic nomination went to Vice President

Hubert Humphrey and the Republican nomination went to Richard Nixon.

When Johnson declined to run again, John Kennedy's brother, Robert Kennedy, seized the opportunity to run for president. He was another charismatic politician with great credentials. During the 1960s and 1970s, Robert Kennedy, played an important role in trying to eliminate some of the terrible racial tensions that were erupting in various cities and on campuses throughout the country. He frequently sent in the National Guard and federal troops and went into those areas himself to try to urge peace. He was a true friend of the Black community, and they knew they could depend on him. Eugene McCarthy did not have national appeal despite his anti-war beliefs. It was no surprise, therefore, that in the presidential election of 1968, Robert Kennedy was as a very strong candidate.

But then, after Kennedy's victory speech when winning the California democratic primary election, at the Los Angeles head-quarters for the Democratic party, he was assassinated by a young Middle Eastern man, Sirhan Sirhan, who was furious at Kennedy's strong support for Israel. This was barely two months after April 4, 1968, and the assassination of Martin Luther King, Jr. What had happened to my country?

I want to comment on this a little. At no time in our history has something like this occurred. Martin Luther King was assassinated on April 4, 1968, and now on June 5, 1968, Robert Kennedy was also assassinated. How could this be in America? A country in which we have laws. If you did not like the position of a candidate, you voted against him. We did not have a history of making changes in political ideology by murdering our opponents. To have these assassinations within a few months of each other was startling.

George Wallace, the governor of Alabama, joined the presidential race as a third-party candidate. The popular vote in the election was very close. Richard Nixon, the Republican candidate won by 500,000 votes. The terrible thing about the election was that George Wallace, a strong segregationist, carried five southern states and ten million votes. The racist attitude of many Americans was very strong and the vote for Wallace unfortunately was evidence of this. Wallace's rise was a direct result of President Johnson's support for and enactment of the 1965 Voting Rights Act. Johnson knew that passing the Voting Rights Act lost the South for the Democratic party. Nixon won assuring Americans that he had a way of ending the Vietnam War.

Nixon took office in January 1969. There were many violent demonstrations. Without Martin Luther King, Jr. there seemed to be no leader in the Black community. Antiwar protests and civil rights protests continued and were held largely on college campuses. At the same time, the US economy was suffering, the cost of living was high, and unemployment and inflation were rising. And the war in Vietnam continued to be a crisis issue.

Nixon kept saying that he had a way to get us out of the war. In March of 1969, Nixon's secretary of defense, Melvin Laird, announced that the president's plan to end the United States involvement was something he called Vietnamization. Under this plan, US troops would be replaced by South Vietnamese soldiers. Nixon kept saying that the number of US forces would be reduced by the end of his first term, but this was a strategy that would take at least four more years of US involvement in Vietnam. This plan was not acceptable to most of the antiwar protesters. When Nixon took office, there were over 500,000 American soldiers and advisors in Vietnam. To his credit, by 1972, that number was reduced to 69,000. But there were other costs for this troop reduction.

Nixon's strategy also included a massive increase in the bombing of North Vietnam. This included the use of 135,000 tons of explosives a month. You can be sure that the antiwar protesters did not accept this. As Jim Callan writes:

The third part of the plan was secret. The CIA led a mission called Operation Phoenix to eliminate the Viet Cong from South Vietnam. Over the next four years Operation Phoenix would kill at least 20,000 Vietnamese who were suspected of being Viet Cong supporters. Even though US troops were to be slowly withdrawn, Nixon was also trying to win the war. Just as Johnson felt before him, Nixon did not want to be the first US president to lose a war.[6]

The first 25,000 US troops left Vietnam in the summer of 1969. One hundred thousand more soldiers came home at the end of 1969, but the war continued.

The US was bombing North Vietnamese bases in Cambodia. North Vietnam had been launching attacks on US troops from those posts in Cambodia. In 1970, Nixon announced that American troops would enter Cambodia, but the air strikes remained a secret for four years. During that time, 100,000 Cambodians were killed and two million were left homeless.

Paris Peace Talks had been set up to find some solution to the Vietnam War. Nothing seemed to go right in those negotiations.

Student protests grew very angry at Nixon's Vietnam policy. Violent groups started to come on the scene such as the Weathermen, who were dedicated to bringing down the government. These revolutionary activities became "the days of rage." A solution to Vietnam could help stop the violence that these protests were producing.

Throughout 1969, the National Guard was called in frequently to stem the violence on college campuses, as young people were increasingly angered by the state of the nation. They were also angered by the lottery draft. There were terrible riots at the University of Wisconsin, Duke University, and the University of California at Berkeley. My law school alma mater Columbia University had an event in 1968 that shut down the campus and made a hero out of student activist Mark Rudd. Even at Harvard, 200 students were arrested calling for the removal of the ROTC group from the campus. Students in twenty-three states took over campuses and had demonstrations that resulted in many, many arrests. The worst demonstration occurred at Kent State University in Ohio in May 1970. Tragically, National Guard soldiers opened fire on students protesting the war, killing four students and wounding eight others. It seemed to me that there was no end in sight to the violence and, as a nation, we were all incredibly disheartened.

chapter six

From AJC to NYU

———★———

The 1970s gave America a new word, "Watergate." This a word that reminds Americans that presidents lie, that people in the highest echelons of government lie, that politicians will break the law to win an election, and that even presidents will break the law. If the 1970s did nothing else, it left us with that word, a word that symbolized the disillusionment we underwent during those critical years, attitudes that lingered on in many of the years to come. And, now with President Trump lying over 30,000 times since he came into office, Watergate seems so innocent.

Still, the word Watergate had not yet become a part of our lexicon in the early 1970s. The war in Vietnam remained at the center of US politics as the decade began. The situation was getting worse and worse. While college students were becoming more hostile to the war, morale within the army was also dropping precipitously.

The US commander in Vietnam was General William Westmoreland. His army was now composed of young men who had been drafted into the army; they were not volunteers. They had not chosen to enroll but had been picked by lottery. They were fighting in a jungle where the enemy could be anywhere. The reasons for the war seemed increasingly obscure to the general public, and soldiers were unsure why they were fighting in the first place. Spirits were very low, life was an ordeal, and drugs and other stimulants made it more livable.

The young men from the working class, the children of the poor, were by and large the ones carrying the burden of the war, while college students were exempt from the draft. These students had the luxury to protest while the poor did not. It was a sad situation and, as time moved on, it was not getting better.

At home, a counterculture had developed. Protesters had long hair and embraced drugs, free love, and their own style of music—rock and roll. As the war progressed, they became more aggressive, greeting returning soldiers with jeers and taunts. Thus, the number of demonstrations against the war increased and became even more violent. On July 24, 1971, approximately 500,000 people marched in Washington, DC in opposition to the war. Smaller protests occurred weekly at colleges and universities around the country. Many veteran groups began taking part in the movement, helping to strengthen the antiwar opposition. The United States government finally came to realize that remaining at war in Vietnam was a "no win" situation.

President Nixon and his administration began seriously making plans to withdraw US troops. Still, morale in the Army continued to get worse. Americans were still dying and thousands more were injured. It mattered not that Kennedy, Johnson, and Nixon all said they would not be the president of a country that lost a war to Communists. The fact was that the United States had already lost the war in Vietnam, and they had lost it to Communists, albeit nationalists whose aim was a united Vietnam. Even after the United States began withdrawing its soldiers, the process was a slow one. After the establishment of a cease-fire on January 27, 1973, US soldiers began leaving Vietnam at a quicker pace, and for good. A peace conference was set up to begin negotiations to end the war.

The Vietnam War was the longest war in United States history. For the US, the Vietnam War began on November 1, 1955, and ended on April 30, 1975. Nixon's Secretary of State, Henry Kissinger, and Le Duc Tho, special adviser to the North Vietnamese delegation to the Paris Peace talks negotiated the ceasefire and were subsequently selected for the 1973 Nobel Peace Prize. Mr. Tho declined the honor.

Despite the fact that there was much criticism of Nixon's role in the war, he had soundly defeated George McGovern in the 1972 presidential election and won a second term. Towards the end of his campaign for the presidency, a group of burglars broke into the headquarters of the Democratic party, which were located in the Watergate Hotel and Office Complex. They planned to put wiretaps in the office to eavesdrop on what the Democratic campaign workers were saying. The burglars were caught. But the story was bigger than the burglary. Two reporters for the *Washington Post*, Bob Woodward and Carl Bernstein, broke the story, which showed that high ranking government officials were involved in the break-in. The incident quickly became international news. Woodward and Bernstein were able to break the full story due to tips they received from an informant called "Deep Throat." Thirty years later, in June 2005, Deep Throat revealed himself to be Mark Felt, a former number two official in the FBI.

Still, in the early days of the scandal, the Nixon administration denied knowledge of the break-in. But soon it became clear that the Nixon administration did indeed know about the Watergate break-in and had tried to cover it up. Nixon's campaign had a fundraising committee called the Committee to Reelect the president (popularly known as CREEP). J. Gordon Liddy headed this committee, and it was under the auspices of the

United States Attorney General John Mitchell. Before long it was obvious that the Watergate break-in was tied to this committee. As investigations continued, reporting revealed that the cover up of the Watergate break-in involved many high-ranking officials. This included White House Counsel John Dean, Assistant to the President for Domestic Affairs John Ehrlichman, and Nixon's chief of staff Harry Robbin Haldeman. Included in the Watergate fiasco was the fact that Nixon's henchmen had burglarized the office of Danial Ellsberg's psychiatrist. Mr. Ellsberg was a senior official at the Rand Corporation and secretly released the government's history in Vietnam to *The New York Times*, soon to be called The Pentagon Papers.

In Senate hearings, a witness told senators that President Nixon had secretly taped conversations in the Oval Office. The Senate demanded those tapes. The president and his chief assistants continued to deny involvement. Congress found it necessary to investigate what role Watergate might have played in the 1972 election. The Senate Select Committee on Presidential Campaign Activities began public hearings on May 17, 1973.

In March 1974, a federal grand jury indicted seven associates of President Nixon for conspiracy to obstruct justice and other offenses leading to the Watergate burglary. The president himself was named as a co-conspirator, but he was not indicted. The Washington, DC district court issued a subpoena commanding the president to testify in court and requiring him to produce certain tapes and papers relating to meetings between himself and others. Nixon refused to turn in these tapes on the grounds of executive privilege. Chief Justice Warren Burger reaffirmed the ruling that under the Constitution the courts have the final voice in determining constitutional questions. This means that not even the president of the United States is above the law. The tapes were ordered to be given to the district court as its subpoena requested.

On August 5, 1974, transcripts of sixty-four tape recordings were released, including one that was particularly damaging.

The tape recordings showed that Nixon participated in the Watergate cover up beginning in June 1972. He suggested paying the Watergate burglars to keep them from talking, ordered illegal wiretaps, used campaign funds illegally, and directed the FBI to stop the investigation.

Never before has a United States president been so exposed to public scrutiny. The tapes not only laid bare evidence of wrongdoing with regard to Watergate but also revealed unflattering aspects of Nixon's personality, such as tendencies toward vindictiveness and bigotry. The president was facing the prospect of impeachment hearings, and around the country there were calls for him to resign. Three days later, on August 8, knowing that he had no support in Congress, Nixon announced that he would resign. Nineteen White House aides and associates would eventually serve prison terms for their role in the cover up of the Watergate scandal.

Nixon's vice president, Gerald Ford, became president. Upon assuming office, Ford stated, "I have not sought this enormous responsibility, but I will not shirk it. Those who nominated and confirmed me as vice president were my friends and are my friends. They were of both parties, elected by all the people and acting under the Constitution in their name. It is only fitting then that I should pledge to them and to you that I will be the president of all the people." He then went on to add, "My fellow Americans, the long national nightmare is over. Our Constitution works. Our great republic is a government of laws and not of men. Here the people rule but there is a higher power. By whatever name we honor Him, He ordains not only righteousness, but love; not only justice, but mercy . . . let us restore the golden rule to our political process and let love purge your hearts of suspicion and hate."[1]

Ford's speech was superb, but morale in the nation was very low. Nonetheless, I want to emphasize that the 1970s were not only a time of political disillusionment in the United States, it was also a decade of progress. In 1973, the Supreme Court handed down one of its most important decisions involving a case called *Roe v. Wade*. In that case, the plaintiff claimed that a Texas statute which made it a crime to perform an abortion unless a woman's life was at stake was unconstitutional. The court sided with Roe, striking down the Texas law. *Roe v. Wade* is the case that effectively legalized abortion nationwide. At the time the decision was handed down, nearly all states outlawed abortion with certain exceptions. *Roe v. Wade* made these laws unconstitutional, making abortion more available to women throughout the country.

At the present time, anti-abortion groups are working state by state to try and undo the protections that *Roe v. Wade* has given to women.[2] I absolutely believe that women in this country who believe that women must have the option to choose must be alert to what the anti-abortion groups are doing. I am in that group of women who support abortion, and I do whatever I can to support the organizations like Planned Parenthood that are supporting *Roe* today.

Another major development in politics at the time occurred on the global stage and hit close to home for me, as I was working at the AJC. I'm speaking, of course, about the Yom Kippur War. In 1967, Egypt and Syria waged a war against Israel. Israel won and gained control of the Sinai Peninsula and Golan Heights. On October 6, 1973, Yom Kippur Day, Egypt and Syria again launched an attack against Israel in an effort to get back the land they lost in 1967. They received help from Saudi Arabia, Jordan, Iraq, Libya, Tunisia, Algeria, Morocco, and Cuba.

The Israelis were in serious need of additional military equipment. They were not ready for this war. In desperation, Golda Meir called Richard Nixon asking for his help in providing military aid to Israel. She did not want to see Israel defeated and did not want to see herself as the last Prime Minister of Israel. She explained to Nixon that she absolutely needed military equipment, and if she did not get that equipment, she might consider using the atom bomb. Nixon felt he had no other choice and sent over all the military machinery that Israel needed and that eventually helped Israel repel Egypt and Syria and win the war. But, Nixon, after sending over the military equipment, said to Meir, "Let's negotiate." Meir and Nixon did exactly that, and the war ended. Without Nixon's pledge to send over military equipment and without Meir threatening to use nuclear weapons, who knows how that war would have come out.

Since I was at the AJC, I was part of a delegation that went to Washington, DC, to congratulate Golda Meir on Israel's victory. She came over to Washington, DC, to thank Nixon. For all Nixon's treachery, this is something that he did that in many ways saved the state of Israel. Nonetheless, his actions here were overshadowed by Watergate.

It's true, Watergate was a catastrophe, but I do want to say here that Nixon did many positive things as president, and yet most people only remember Watergate. For example, he supported the Environmental Protection Agency. He supported occupational and health departments. And, under Nixon's presidency, the United States established relationships with Egypt for the first time since 1967. Not only that, he ended the draft to Vietnam. He visited China and opened the door for better economic and political relations with China. He initiated the Anti-Ballistic Missile Treaty with the Soviet Union in 1973. He enforced desegregation of the schools in the south.

Anyway, at this point in the story, Nixon was out (for good reason), and we now had President Ford. President Gerald Ford was a decent man, not a world beater, but committed to carry out Nixon's efforts to reduce Cold War tensions. He continued negotiations between the Soviet Union and the United States about arms.

One of Ford's first acts was to issue Richard Nixon a pardon on September 9, 1974. This pardon freed Nixon from any crimes he may have committed while he was president. He would not have to face any criminal indictments or stand trial for any crimes in which he may have been involved in relating to Watergate. President Ford announced the pardon in a speech on television. He explained that he made this decision because he did not think Nixon could obtain a fair trial at this point in any court in the United States saying, "I feel that Richard Nixon and his loved ones have suffered enough and will continue to suffer, no matter what I do, no matter what we, as a great and good nation, can do together to make his goal of peace come true."[3] In 2002, Gerald Ford received the John F. Kennedy Profile in Courage Award for his pardon of Richard Nixon.

Whether Ford made a deal with Nixon, agreeing to pardon Nixon if he resigned and let Ford become president, one does not know. It is gossip. That is all.

As I have noted, the United States began to withdraw from Vietnam in 1972 under Nixon and continued this process during the Ford administration. Without American aid, the South Vietnamese Army was not capable of holding back the Communists armies from the North. The northern armies captured the city of Saigon. President Ford offered to air lift anti-Communists, who feared for their lives, out of the city. Most of the refugees were taken to the United States. Americans who were in Saigon were evacuated as the city fell to the invading Viet Cong. In America, we watched our televisions in horror, gripped by the heartbreaking images of emergency helicopters rescuing Americans from the roof of the US Embassy, carrying the evacuees to ships waiting off the coast. Thousands of South Vietnamese tried to join this evacuation and forced their way onto the helicopters that could barely fly due to being weighed down by the people hanging on. After the North Vietnamese entered Saigon, on April 30, 1975, the South Vietnamese president surrendered unconditionally to the Communist North Vietnam.

Over 58,000 American soldiers died in the Vietnam War

and the thousands who returned home were scarred forever by their experiences of the conflict. "The end of the war," President Ford said, "closed a chapter in the American experience."[4] It was, indeed, a sad and, in retrospect, a useless American experience.

For a strange set of reasons, the conflict over the war in Vietnam was directly tied to one of the most significant developments in my life. This was that, in 1972, I became the National Executive Director of the AJC—the only woman to hold such a position in a Jewish organization that had within it both men and women. It shocks me to say this, but today—nearly fifty years since then—there has not been another woman to hold such a position in a major, co-ed Jewish organization.[5] It is an outrage. There are women CEOs of some major corporations. There are women presidents of major universities. There are women governors and members of Congress. There were six women running for president of the United States in 2019. And yet, still, not a single woman heads a major Jewish organization. I put some of the blame on the women donors of those organizations. They should make it clear that their financial contributions depend on the organizations looking into this issue seriously.

But anyway, becoming the national executive director of American Jewish Congress—let me tell that story because, here, too, it was something I didn't plan and happened by pure accident. In 1972, Will Maslow, who had been the executive director, announced his retirement.

He wanted to write. He had so many interests. A search committee was set up to find his replacement. On that committee, there were four women. The women in the American Jewish Congress were strongly opposed to the Vietnam War and participated in various protests, meetings, marches, etc. They had sons who were affected by the draft. They saw the futility of being involved in a war of nationalism. The man who was Will

Maslow's assistant director, Richard Cohen, was expected to be his successor. Richard was highly qualified for the position, but he supported the war in Vietnam because he was a believer in the domino theory espoused by President Eisenhower. According to the domino theory, if Vietnam fell to the Communists, the rest of Southeast Asia would become Communist, and this would be bad for the United States and the world at large. The women on the search committee would not vote for Richard Cohen. They opposed the domino theory; they opposed the Vietnam War; they opposed anyone who supported the war in any fashion. Week after week, the committee met, but they only argued.

Finally, Will had enough.

"Let's give it to Naomi Levine on a temporary basis," he said.

The women loved that, they voted for it, and I became the director. They did not know my opinion of the war because on this subject I had been relatively silent. At that time, my brother David worked at the State Department. I viewed David as the smartest man I knew, and he and members of the State Department supported the domino theory, so every time I listened to him, I was persuaded. On the other hand, I saw the antiwar side clearly. I questioned our involvement in the war and had mixed feelings about the entire situation. Because of my internal uncertainty, I never expressed myself publicly about the war in Vietnam. The women never knew my position, and I believe I never would have become the executive director if they knew the truth. I did not lie, but I never openly discussed my conflicted position on Vietnam.

This is another example of the collection of lucky accidents that have been so much a part of my life. If I believed in some spiritual figure that was up above directing me that would be an answer, but since I don't believe in spiritual figures, I have to blame it all on accidents—a foolish response to questions I really cannot answer.

Woman to Head Jewish Congress

New York Post 3/1/72

By LINDSY VAN GELDER

The American Jewish Congress today appointed Naomi Levine, a New York attorney, as executive director. She is the first woman to head a major national Jewish organization of both men and women.

"I must confess I'd like to think I got the job on merit," said Mrs. Levine, a member of the Congress staff for 21 years. "On the other hand, I must admit that five years ago it would have been inconceivable for a woman to be appointed, regardless of merit."

Mrs. Levine — who also serves as assistant professor of race relations at the John Jay College of Criminal Justice and as a consultant to [the] Ford Foundation's Social Development Dept.—will assume her new post Oct. 1, succeeding Will Maslow, who has held the job for 12 years.

In an interview yesterday in her office at 15 E. 84th St., Mrs. Levine said that her main field of concentration in the Congress had been urban affairs — especially the ways that "the law can be used as an important weapon for social change."

Her contributions to the Congress have included organizing projects to advance black capitalism and to help blacks buy ghetto stores from whites. Along with Richard Cohen, she wrote a study of the 1968 Ocean Hill-Brownsville school dispute, and she recently compiled a pamphlet to aid the aged in finding available city services.

Mrs. Levine noted with pride that in addition to its concerns with Jewish culture, social change, urban affairs and world Jewry, the Congress had organizationally condemned the war in Vietnam.

She sees "no conflict" between this stance and advocating U. S. support of Israel. "Israel is a democracy prepared to defend itself, and it's not asking for American troops."

She is particularly concerned with building a coalition of blacks, Jews and others to "improve the city —after all, we all want the same things," and last fall she organized a conference of policemen and minority groups to discuss common efforts to fight crime.

The problem with me and this organization," she laughed, "is that we're reasonable. I believe that a good political process is one that attempts to find compromises between opposing views. Unfortunately, this isn't dramatic or exciting. If I told you I wanted to put a match to something or throw a bomb, that would make a good story."

Mrs. Levine added that she was "particularly disturbed about some of the television coverage of the Forest Hills situation. Every night on the screen I see the extremists, when the truth is that I know several groups who are working behind the scenes to effect some kind of workable solution."

For the same reason, she deplores the "terror tactics" of the Jewish Defense League.

"I don't approve of violence or extreme rhetoric," she said. "It only exacerbates conditions and it doesn't solve any problems. You can be very popular if you go into a neighborhood to organize vigilantes to fight crime. Well, if you're in Dodge City in 1874, that's effective. But it's utterly childish to think that's going to work today in a complex urban situation like New York City."

A graduate of Hunter College and Columbia Law School, Mrs. Levine briefly practiced law but found the field discriminatory against women.

Mrs. Levine said that although she was "screaming" of certain elements of the women's liberation movement, "most of their points are valid, and I endorse them." She also said that "there are many things in Jewish law — divorce, for example — that discriminate against women" and that the Congress has a committee at work on the subject.

Married to Leonard Levine, an accountant, Mrs. Levine has a 22-year-old daughter, Joan, who recently was graduated from NYU. "She's a very liberated young lady, cut much more of the pattern of Gloria Steinem than of her mother," she laughed. Mrs. Levine added that she didn't resent the "Jewish mother" stereotype "as long as its Molly Golberg and not Mrs. Portnoy."

NAOMI LEVINE
Takes over Oct. 1

A selection of press clippings announcing my appointment as National Executive Director of the AJC (Page 111, New York Post; Page 112, Baltimore Sun; and Page 113, Los Angeles Herald Examiner).

She Scores A First For Women As Executive Director Of AJC

By Maxyne B. Trompeter

Women's liberation has helped break down another barrier. The new executive director of the American Jewish Congress is facile, fiftyish and the first female ever to hold this position.

Mrs. Leonard Levine, who will officially take office October 1 replacing Will Maslow, director for the past 12 years, came to Baltimore last week to "talk business" with the Baltimore chapter, AJC. "I'm out to get a better picture of our own grass roots organizations," Mrs. Levine said of the 300 to 400 AJC units scattered across the United States. "I like to change things if I can improve them. Right now I'm looking for people who are committed to the congress and people with contacts who can help increase our membership," she said.

75,000 Members

As head of the staff of one of the largest Jewish defense organizations in the United States, Naomi Levine will be responsible for the work of 75,000 members scattered

throughout the 18 regional offices.

"It's a hard job," she said, "But I can do it. I've been a hard worker all my life, why should it be any different this time?"

She strongly feels that women's liberation has helped her to attain her new position. "Although I'm not happy with its extreme reheteric, the women's lib movement has made it more acceptable to be a working woman. I must admit that five years ago it would have been inconceivable for a woman to be appointed to this position. Women's lib has helped to change all that."

A graduate of Hunter College and Columbia Law School, Mrs. Levine became involved with the AJC as a lawyer interested in civil rights.

That was 21 years ago. Today, she serves as assistant professor of race relations at the John Jay College of Criminal Justice and as a consultant to the Ford Foundation's Social Development Department.

"I'm afraid I'll have to give up some of this," she lamented, "because my new job will keep me busy 40 hours a day."

Religion And War

While the AJC takes firm positions on issues such as religion in schools ("We believe in separation of church and state") and the war in Vietnam ("We maintain a peace position"), the congress cannot support a political candidate at any level.

"Personally, I can support whomever I want," she noted, "But I'm not here to discuss that and I wouldn't tell you anyway."

Politics, she says, attracts her, but she would be afraid of going into active politics "because a politician cannot say what he or she thinks and be successful."

Success, she defined, "is finding satisfaction in how you are living your life. I'm quite satisfied," she said of her marriage for the past 26 years to accountant Leonard Levine and of her professional life.

FIRST FEMALE—Mrs. Leonard Levine will take office October 1 as the first female executive director of AJC.

The mother of a 23-year-old graduate of New York University, Mrs. Levine notes that she has "always wanted to be more than just a wife and mother."

"My own mother didn't want me to continue with graduate school because she said it would make me too smart and nobody would marry me. But my husband did, and all my life I have been struggling successfully to combine my family life and my working life."

Life, she says "is a succession of little accidents. I never really knew I wanted to go into law until I was into it.

Raising Sights

"Law has opened enormous doors for me and it can for any woman. It's an excellent discipline, a good career and can lead down many different roads— government work, teaching, administration or organization work.

Mrs. Levine maintains that women must "raise their sights academically and in careers. We must not be satisfied with the standard careers of nursing and teaching."

Asked if she had hope that her daughter, who will be studying medieval history at Harvard this fall, will go into law, Mrs. Levine replied "I'm too smart to want to choose a direction for my daughter. It's her life, she has to decide how she wants to live it."

Following this visit to Baltimore, the Levines planned to spend the weekend relaxing in the northern Adirondacks. "That's the place to be," she sighed. "You can wear jeans and just be yourself. You don't have to worry about your image."

July 15/72

Dear Naomi,

Have fun!

Will

Naomi Levine of New York City is the first woman to head the staff of a major national Jewish organization of both men and women. In her capacity as National Executive Director of the American Jewish Congress, she was among top leaders to address a special meeting of the Southern California Division at Sinai Temple. She is Assistant Professor of Race Relations at John Jay College of Criminal Justice of the City University and a consultant to the Department of Social Development at the Ford Foundation.

A Los Angeles Herald-Examiner, Tuesday, July 11, 1972

Naomi — For your scrapbook. Best, Herb Brin

Women's World

———

Whatever the reason for my getting the job, the press's reaction to the news of my appointment was extraordinary. There wasn't a paper in the country that did not carry a story about a woman becoming the national executive director of a Jewish organization that contained both men and women. My appointment was even put in the Congressional record.

The next few years were marvelous for me. I loved being national executive director and I loved the many issues the American Jewish Congress was involved in, such as the causes of Israel, Soviet Jewry, the Arab boycott, Jewish education, civil rights, sit-ins, bus wars, marches. I also liked and respected very much the people that I worked with; they were brilliant rabbis, lawyers, and activist women. This was an extraordinary group of people—I found them smarter and more interesting than the many of the academics I met at NYU. They were not only treasured professional colleagues, but in most cases became beloved friends.

I accepted a great many invitations to speak all over the country, in addition to speaking at our chapters. During this period, I also wrote three books, one on Ocean Hill Brownsville (covering the confrontation between New York City's teachers' union and the community-controlled school board in the primarily black New York City neighborhood), another about problems in nursing homes entitled *The Last Resort*, and a book about the Jewish poor. In addition, I continued to write at least one article every week for the AJC biweekly. I went to Israel two to four times a year, as if the Israelis needed my advice as they developed their young country. I worked all the time. Relations between Leonard and me suffered greatly as a result of my constant work and frequent absences.

Still, I loved my job, and so I would like to take the time to comment on a few items that I was especially involved in at

Congressional Record

United States of America

PROCEEDINGS AND DEBATES OF THE 92^d CONGRESS, SECOND SESSION

Vol. 118   WASHINGTON, WEDNESDAY, MARCH 1, 1972   No. 30

AMERICAN JEWISH CONGRESS NAMES NAOMI BRONHEIM LEVINE AS EXECUTIVE DIRECTOR

(Mrs. ABZUG asked and was given permission to address the House for 1 minute and to revise and extend her remarks and include extraneous matter.)

Mrs. ABZUG. Mr. Speaker, the American Jewish Congress has chosen as its new executive director one of this country's outstanding women, a good friend of mine for many years. Naomi-Bronheim Levine today becomes the first woman to lead a major Jewish organization of both men and women, and her appointment is another indication of the progress women are making in every field. I am especially pleased at this timely announcement since Mrs. Levine is a colleague and very dear friend of mine from Hunter College and Columbia Law School. I can vouch for her competence, energy, and enthusiasm in everything she undertakes, and I congratulate the American Jewish Congress for its excellent choice. I have here an article on the appointment from today's New York Times and I include it at this point in the RECORD:

NEW JEWISH LEADER: NAOMI BRONHEIM LEVINE

When Naomi Bronheim Levine was growing up in the Bronx she had a lisp and later, after college, it kept her from becoming a schoolteacher.

But it was a challenge to overcome, as she was to overcome the challenge of combining a career with family. She succeeded with both, and yesterday Mrs. Levine, wife and mother, was appointed executive director of the American Jewish Congress, the first woman to head the staff of a major Jewish organization of both men and women.

Her appointment was, she said, "a complete surprise," but the job itself, directing the work of about 75,000 members scattered throughout 18 regional offices and 300 chapters, was something she was sure she could handle. "I'm not a particularly modest person," Mrs. Levine said.

Mrs. Levine is tough but feminine, able and articulate, yet she is afraid to go into politics, which attracts her, because, she said, a politician cannot say what he or she thinks and be successful. And, she acknowledged, she does went to be successful.

RESPONSIBILITY FOR FAMILY

Philosophically, she bridges the time when women first became seriously career-minded and today's "women's liberation" movement.

"Women's lib is probably correct, but it's not my style," she said.

"I still feel somewhat guilty when I spend too much time away from home and if my daughter got sick I would say home and care for her—I wouldn't expect my husband to. The young girls today think differently and they're right."

Nonetheless, because she is a successful career woman—not despite the fact—she has had to work harder than most perhaps at her marriage of 23 years to Leonard Levine, an accountant.

"There have been problems, but we share many things at home, and we've never had to discuss my working much," she says. "We just do and help each other."

"He lets me handle the social problems of the world and he makes the money," Mrs. Levine says of her husband. "What I do is very important to me, and I could have life no other way."

The couple have a daughter, Joan, 23, a recent graduate of New York University, who has an apartment in Greenwich Village. Miss Levine, who plans to become a teacher, said yesterday that she could not recall having ever suffered from having a successful mother.

"I always looked up to her and thought of her as a brilliant woman," she continued. "It's hard for me to imagine a woman who didn't have a career. She made me look to a career. There are a lot of men frightened of such a woman, but my father is obviously not one of them."

Naomi Bronheim was born on April 18, 1923, the daughter of Mr. and Mrs. Nat Bronheim. Her younger brother, David, was director of the Alliance for Progress under President John F. Kennedy and was a director of the Center of Inter-American Affairs.

Mrs. Levine attended Hunter College High School, one of the most difficult to get into, and then Hunter College, from which she graduated in 1940, intending to become a public school teacher. "I passed the written exam, but failed the oral because of my lisp," she recalled.

A teacher suggested that she go to law school instead, and so she enrolled at Columbia. She graduated in 1944 and was an editor of the Law Review.

Only for a short period of time did she engage in private law practice. "But there, you see, I felt guilty about the time I was taking away from my family so I quit."

Mrs. Levine, who has been at the American-Jewish Congress for 21 years, succeeds Will Maslow as executive director. Mr. Maslow served in the post for 12 years and will continue as general counsel.

PROFESSOR AT JOHN JAY

Mrs. Levine's only major regret about her new job, she said, is that she will have to give up her professorship at the John Jay College of Criminal Justice where, for four years, she has been teaching policemen about law and race relations and the American judicial system.

Her minor regret is the prospect of flying, which she hates. As executive director of an organization with an annual budget of $2.5-million she will, in her new job, have to do a lot of traveling to speak and raise funds.

Mrs. Levine and her husband live in a seven-room apartment on West End Avenue and 85th Street.

Her hobbies are reading and going to the theater. Recently she hired two young scholars at Yeshiva University to give her private tutoring in Jewish history, all of which proves, her husband says, is that she is extravagant."

Entry regarding my new position at the AJC in the Congressional Record.

the AJC during these years. One was that I orchestrated many meetings with representatives of *60 Minutes*, a CBS program, because the AJC felt strongly that *60 Minutes* had developed an episode on Syrian Jews that we believed was filled with errors and distortions. After many of our meetings they revised the program and showed the revised program at another date. We were very pleased about this.

I also worked closely with Richard Cohen, the associate executive director of the American Jewish Congress, on our program against the Arab Boycott, i.e. the fact that Arab nations were boycotting Israel. The AJC suggested a new federal bill that we drafted to outlaw cooperation with companies involved in the boycott. We also, in a twenty-nine-page legal memo, called on President Ford to invoke existing federal law against boycott pressures that were then being directed at American companies. At a news conference, we made our position and memo public. We underscored that there were eight federal statutes already on the books that made many aspects of the boycott illegal. The government had enough cause to bring legal action in this field. In summary, we said that the United States should not tolerate restrictions on free trade and should not permit the boycott or discrimination to interfere with the flow of commerce in our country or the world.

Lois Waldman, one of the lawyers in our Commission on Law and Social Action, had a good idea about how to further our efforts in this area. She suggested that we buy one or two shares of stock in those companies that were participating in the boycott and, at one of their board meetings, since we were stockholders, we could raise this issue and get the company to discuss it. We did this—buying one or two shares of stock in many of those companies—and then attending many of these companies' board meetings and raising the issue. In many cases, their stockholders agreed with us, and, in some cases, we changed their company's position on the Arab boycott. I can say without hesitation that the AJC played a major role in the fight against the Arab boycott, and I was proud to be part of it.

In addition, one of the most interesting projects in which I was involved in my new role was the Interracial Council for Business Opportunity (ICBO). This initiative began when a group of businessmen including, Rodman Rockefeller, the eldest son of the governor Nelson Rockefeller of New York (Nelson Rockefeller became Gerald Ford's vice president), came to me with an idea (the other members of this group were Al Lasher, Allen Rosenberg, and a few others). They felt that Jewish businessmen had a long history of being very involved and successful in business. They thought that Jewish business owners could be of help to the Black community, and they wanted to form an alliance between Jewish and Black business owners to help Black people succeed in business.

Their project would be to ask businessmen in the AJC to work with the Black community to provide help to Black businesses that felt they needed help. I thought the idea was a very good one, and since Rodman Rockefeller was deeply involved, we thought we had a good chance of getting funding from the Rockefeller Foundation. We were right. We got our funding from the Rockefeller Foundation. We also believed the initiative would bring in more businessmen to the American Jewish Congress and thus it would help strengthen our membership, in addition to deepening our relations with the Black community.

Indeed, the reaction from the Black community was very favorable. In a year or two, when we went back to Rockefeller for more money, they did a study of the ICBO and concluded that it was one of the most important projects undertaken to help the Black community. The foundation gave us money for additional work, and during the next few years the project was so successful that it was adopted by the federal government. I believe it still exists today, funded and supervised by the federal government. Until the federal government took over, I was the director of the ICBO, since it was part of the AJC program activities, and I was always very proud of my involvement in this project.

Leonard and I at an AJC Gala.

As I briefly mentioned before, during my time as national executive director of the American Jewish Congress, Rae Weiss was my secretary. As for Rae Weiss, I would not know where to begin. She served as my secretary and administrative aide for twenty-five years at AJC. She went on to NYU and served with me for another twenty-five years. At the AJC, she worked all day from 8 a.m. to 6 or 7 p.m. every weekday and sometimes on weekends. She traveled with me, as I found it hard to go around by myself due my psychological issues. She was almost mugged in her apartment on King's Highway one year, so Leonard and I bought her a studio in Brighton Beach.

During the last years of her life, her vision started to go, and Leonard and I let her live in our maid's room at 29 Washington

Square West. On the last day of her life, we had to move her into a hospital. While in the hospital, she asked to hold my hand and told me to go to her apartment in Brooklyn and get her Gristede's bag. (Gristede's is an iconic New York City grocery store). I told her I had to go to class, as I was teaching that night. I asked my other secretary, Bonnie Burns, to take her hand and Bonnie did so. When the class was over, I called the hospital and was told that Rae had died.

That weekend I took five people, including my housekeeper, two maintenance men I knew, and some friends, and went to clean out her apartment in Brighton Beach, as Leonard was eager to sell it as soon as possible.

It was a mess. We spent about three hours collecting garbage of one sort or another into huge garbage bags. At the door when we were about to leave, I realized I had forgotten to look for the Gristede's bag. Everyone thought I was crazy when I insisted we go back and look for the bag in the garbage. But I held fast, for reasons I will never know. I said they could leave and that I would do it myself. They were not going to let me do the job alone so they all volunteered again to help me. In the sixth bag, underneath costume jewelry, we found $649,300 in federal bonds.

We could not believe what we saw. In all the time that Rae lived with me, Leonard and I paid for everything. We hired a health aide to help her dress; we took her to restaurants or brought food for her. Never did she offer to pay one penny. At AJC, when she was working for me, she had one or two simple dresses and never wore anything that looked like it cost any money. When we traveled together, I paid for everything. Who can explain people's relationship to money? And who can explain all the mysteries that make up a life? What made me go back and search for the bag? Everyone who was with me on the precipice of her apartment in Brighton Beach reminded me that Rae was half in a coma when she made that request, and yet I insisted on going back for no rational reason to look for that Gristede's bag. If I was a religious person, I would call it a "message from God," but I'm not. All I can do is call it a mystery and leave it at that.

When Rae died, my lawyer Herb Paul had a letter she had left with him to be opened at her death. The letter was addressed to me and said: "I loved you more than anyone in the world and you treated me like a typewriter." In that letter, she went on to explain that she was a lesbian and wanted very much to have a more intimate relationship with me and, because my marriage was going through difficult times, she thought there was a possibility of such a relationship.

I must confess, I never noticed anything she did that I would classify as a pass. Again, it's a mystery. But I was so involved in my work, I probably never noticed what was going on personally around me. I often think, "What would I have done if I had found out how she felt?" Part of me says I would have fired her. The other part says no, I would have talked to her, told her that I could not meet what she wanted, and she could stay if she understood that. In any event, she died, and we never had such a discussion. The only thing that remains is her poignant letter opened on the day she died.

—

Despite my obsession with my work and the difficulties this caused in my relationship with Leonard, the beginning of the 1970s signaled a wonderful change for us. We bought our first house in Westport, CT. This was how it happened: One day, coming home from Fire Island, Leonard to our surprise exclaimed, "I am not going to suffer in this traffic again." It's true that traffic was awful on the Long Island Expressway on Sunday nights. After his outburst, we sold our home on Fire Island. Because my best friend, Betty Warshaw, had a home in Westport we started to look for a second home in that area of Connecticut.

So, in 1972, with Betty Warshaw's help, Leonard and I bought our first home in Westport, Connecticut. Westport is about one hour from New York City and is a very lovely community on Long Island Sound. It has both water and beautiful countryside. Our first home in Westport was on the Saugatuck River, with a beautiful, great lawn stretching from the back of the house to the river. My grandchildren, Chloé and Olivia, were very young at that point and loved to play in the river.

Betty Warshaw had many friends, and Leonard and I joined the group. Every Friday night we would meet Betty and her friends at the Sherwood Diner and eat dinner together. They included Mildred and Herbert Abrams, Jeanne and Budgie (Leo) Gordon, Betty and Dr. Hank Corwin, Betty and Mal Warshaw, Leonard and me. There was no poker, but the conversation was always great. There was always a party over the weekend. These were very intelligent people who shared our political beliefs, and we had a great time with them. Westport was known for having a very theatrical, artistic, left-leaning community. In addition to great people, it also has good restaurants and the Westport Playhouse.

Several years later, we sold that house in Westport and bought a bigger house with its own swimming pool that our grandchildren enjoyed very much. It was within walking distance from Compo Beach.

So, I had an active social life in Westport an even more active one thanks to the AJC. Of all the friends I made during my time at the AJC, Dr. Arthur Hertzberg was one of the dearest. Rabbi Hertzberg was the president of the American Jewish Congress during my tenure. He summarized our relationship beautifully in his book, *A Jew in America*. He wrote,

> The new executive director was Naomi Levine, the first woman to be appointed to such a post in any national organization in which the membership was predominantly male. I soon discovered several things about Naomi: she was nervous about her new job, and she had

been told that I was difficult to work with because I was opinionated and probably a male chauvinist: but only the first charge was true.

She made it clear to me from the beginning that she was a committed Jew, but did not believe in God. She was challenging me, the rabbi, to persuade her that he (or she) existed. What she never told me directly I found out almost immediately. She possessed a brilliant mind and an unfailing sense of the difference between right and wrong. Naomi and I very quickly drifted into the habit of spending an hour or two in her office or mine arguing about God and matters of organizational policy. I remember the day that all the pre-existing barriers fell. I looked at Naomi one day and said to her that I do not believe that brains have gender—and at that moment we became not only colleagues, but devoted friends.[6]

Indeed, it was exactly as Arthur told it. He and I were very good friends. However, few people in the American Jewish Congress liked him. As a rule, he did not make friends easily. He was a difficult and arrogant, but brilliant man. If he had a different personality, he would have been the "King of the Jews" because no one matched him in his brilliance. When he ran for president for a second term, something that presidents of the American Jewish Congress always did, he was defeated by a young lawyer, Howard Squadron (yes, the same young man from my neighborhood in the Bronx whose mother-in-law leant me the schlock money for Camp Greylock almost two decades before). Howard was the first president of the American Jewish Congress who was not a rabbi. The AJC always had a rabbi as a president to underscore our commitment to Judaism. I was very upset by Howard's election. Although I knew him from the neighborhood and law school, and I liked him and respected his brilliance and commitment to the American Jewish Congress, I continued to believe that a rabbi should be the face of the organization. I took this position because the AJC at this time was deeply involved in the civil rights struggle, and I feared its Jewish component was being lost. I believed that because the AJC was viewed throughout the country as a Jewish organization with emphasis on civil rights, the Jewish component of our work was less visible as we became more and more involved in civil rights. A rabbi in the post as president reaffirmed our commitment to Jewish issues and was one way of the AJC saying "yes, we are a strong civil rights organization, but we are also Jewish." But the organization felt differently, and Howard Squadron was elected president, almost unanimously. Howard turned out to be a very good president.

Lone woman (I'm second to the back, on the right)

Tied to this issue was another one that soured me a little. The AJC never had a great deal of money and a good portion of our money in the 1970s went for our work in civil rights. We, as stated before, worked closely with minority communities on the theory that if any country treated their Black community the way the US treated the Black community, then Jews would be next. During that time, several of our members felt that we should use some of the money from the civil rights program to create a commission on Jewish education. They believed that it was important that a Jewish organization have programs to help Jews to understand the values of Judaism and why people have died for thousands of years to support it. Most Jews unfortunately are Jewishly illiterate. They like their lox and bagels and gefilte fish, but they knew very little about Judaism. At the AJC, the debate between these two factions grew more and more intense, and the group that supported the creation of a commission on Jewish education was the victor. Shad and Justine Polier left the American Jewish Congress because of that decision. I was heartsick. The Poliers were strongly in support of major activities in the area of civil rights, and they were unhappy that money would be taken from those programs. For more than twenty years, Justine Polier and I had been both professional and personal friends. I became the executive director of the American Jewish Congress, I believe, because of everything she taught me and her influence among the leaders. I repeat: I was devastated.

That week I was having lunch at the Harmonie Club with Ben Epstein, the executive director of the Anti-Defamation League. I shared with him my unhappiness. I told him that I had a great job at the AJC, which I enjoyed, but after twenty-five years, maybe it was time for me to make a change. I was fifty-five years of age, and if I did not do that at this point in my life, the chances of my ever finding another job were highly unlikely. He told me that there at the Harmonie Club, at another table, was a man named Herb Silverman, who was chairing a search committee for New York University. They were looking for a vice president. Mr. Epstein knew very little about the job opening, but he called Herb Silverman to our table and introduced me to him, explaining my desire to make a change in my employment. Herb took my name

With my mentor, Judge Justine Wise Polier.

to give to the president of NYU. He was very polite, and then left to go back to his own table. I thought nothing would come of that introduction.

To my amazement, when I got back to my office after lunch, there was a call from John Sawhill, who was the president of NYU, asking me to come down to visit him at once. As shocked as I was, I took a cab and went down to NYU. After a fifteen-minute interview, John Sawhill offered me the job and without carefully thinking about what I was embarking on and without talking with my family or colleagues, I accepted his offer and became the senior vice president of New York University. I was appointed in 1978, and I held that position until I retired in 2004.

I could never figure out why John Sawhill offered me the position. But a few years ago, I was in the archives of NYU and found an old memo from John Sawhill to Larry Tisch, chairman of the NYU Board of Trustees, telling him, "I just hired Naomi Levine for the job of senior vice president. She will be responsible for our fundraising. I chose her because she is the executive director of that organization that has within it all the affluent people we want to solicit in our fundraising efforts."

John Sawhill did not know the difference between the American Jewish Committee, which had within it all the affluent Jews in the United States, and the American Jewish Congress in which I worked, which had very few. So once again, luck and an "accident" played a role in my appointment as senior vice president of New York University.

So, I was leading the AJC, and then planning a move to NYU, all the while the American political landscape continued to be enmeshed in turmoil. In 1976, Gerald Ford ran for reelection. He was challenged by the Republican nomination of the California Governor, Ronald Reagan, but Ford gained the vote of just enough delegates at the convention to become the Republican candidate. The president selected former Senator Robert Dole as his running mate. The Democratic nominee was Jimmy Carter, a peanut farmer from Plains, Georgia.

As I read through the material about Carter's presidency, I see how many of Carter's extraordinary accomplishments were overshadowed by the Iran Hostage Crisis. Nothing that he could have done would have made the public feel comfortable with him because they felt he was not effective enough to get the American hostages back.

Carter was a man very different from Nixon. He was very honest, decent, and intelligent—the type of man who spent many a Sunday teaching the Bible in his local church. Originally, the voters found Carter a personable candidate, but most important he was not related to anyone associated with Watergate. He came to Washington a clean, honest man with not a taint of corruption surrounding him. Even though President Ford was not linked directly with Watergate, people still associated him with Nixon because he had served as Nixon's vice president, and because as president he had pardoned Nixon.

Jimmy Carter was elected to the presidency in November of 1976. He beat Ford in one of the closest presidential elections in American history. Carter promised to heal the wounds of Watergate and Vietnam. On his second day in office, Carter pardoned all the Vietnam War draft evaders. In my opinion, his greatest personal achievement involved his efforts to bring peace between Israel and Egypt.

Indeed, during his presidency, President Carter accomplished a great deal. To sum it up, he:

- Established diplomatic relations in trade with China, building on Nixon's efforts
- Transferred control of the Panama Canal
- Worked on nuclear arms control
- Was deeply concerned with international human rights all over the world
- Appointed 265 judges to the federal bench, including many minorities and women
- Appointed more Black people in influential positions in the federal government than any president before him

But the economy in the country was very bad. Overall unemployment was high, social programs were being reduced, and Black unemployment remained in the double digits, twice the rate of unemployment for white Americans. When Carter took office, the unemployment rate had reached a high of 7.7 percent. Indeed, during the '70s, the country saw rising unemployment overall, with many parts of the country facing serious loss of their economic base. The energy crisis and our dependence on oil from foreign sources certainly did not help. Whatever Carter tried to do concerning the economy, it did not work. It only got worse during his four years as president. When unemployment and economic problems begin to face the nation, Black people always seem to bear the burden most of all. In 1971, Jesse Jackson founded PUSH (People United to Save Humanity) in Chicago to help poor people. At the same time, the white community became concerned that affirmative action was helping the Black community at their expense. A backlash against affirmative action, busing, and other efforts to help the Black community began. It was a bad sign.

Congress, on Carter's request, passed an Economic Stimulus Appropriations Act to create jobs. This caused unemployment to decline a little, but huge price hikes in oil from the Middle East doomed his agenda.

So, Carter was faced with an energy crisis that was getting worse and worse. He made energy a top priority. He told the American people that 75 percent of the oil and natural gas that we rely on for energy was running out. Gas lines at gas stations were long.

The basis of President Carter's plan was energy conservation. He urged Americans to conserve energy and to buy equipment that would help them do so, but he also made clear that there was a need for alternative energy sources. He urged Americans to turn down the heat in their homes and wear sweaters. He also pushed for the country to begin to consider solar power. He asked Congress to begin to institute tax credits to reward responsible energy conservation. Tax credits were offered to individuals and businesses to motivate them to insulate their homes, stores, and factories. He lobbied Congress for a tax on gas to reduce gas consumption. He promised a tax on gas guzzler cars. He sought greater production of domestic coal and oil and explored the use of nuclear power plants. He also hoped solar cells, geothermal energy, and wind turbines would become usable alternatives and he pursued federal funding for their development. He was ahead of his time on the energy crisis. None of his suggestions were adopted by the Congress.

During Carter's presidency two new cabinet departments were created: the Department of Energy and the Department of Education. So, he did manage to establish a national energy policy that included conservation, price control, and new technologies.

Carter was never given sufficient credit for all these efforts because of the Iran Hostage Crisis, which I'll describe in a moment. Still, he was truly committed to the causes he believed in. Even after he left the presidency in 1982, he established the Carter Center to promote and expand human rights. He traveled to many countries throughout the world talking about human rights urging that the countries make this a priority and urging governments to move in that direction. He has written over thirty books and continues to be involved in global affairs. In 2002, he was awarded the Nobel Peace Prize for establishing the Carter Center, which continues to play a role in the pursuit of human rights. Jimmy Carter and his wife became avid proponents of Habitat For Humanity, helping to build thousands of homes for those in need.

But of all his admirable efforts, I believe one of the most shining moments in Carter's presidency was the role he played in getting Anwar Sadat and Menachem Begin together at Camp David to try and work out some kind of peace treaty between Egypt and Israel. President Carter recognized that problems in the Middle East would ultimately increase tensions between the United States and the Soviet Union because the Soviet Union was supporting the Arab nations with money and weapons. Carter was also deeply committed to the support of Israel. "The Judaic-Christian effort and study of the Bible were bonds between Jews and Christians which were always a part of my life," Carter stated. "I also believe very deeply that the Jews who survived the Holocaust deserved their own nation and to live in peace."[7]

Carter desperately wanted to help bring about that peace. He believed that bringing Begin and Sadat to Camp David could result in a conversation between the two nations that could ultimately result in a peace treaty. After years as a Soviet ally, Egypt had a failing economy, and regaining the Sinai Peninsula would help immeasurably to boost Egyptians' morale. It would also help Egypt obtain financial support from the United States.

From Israel's perspective, the prospect of peace was an important element of national security. Even before the Camp David

Summit meetings, Sadat visited Israel, and Begin visited Egypt as well, thus indicating that both parties were now more willing to talk and find ways to compromise.

Carter hoped that getting Sadat and Begin to Camp David, away from the press and out of the glare of publicity, would help each to understand the other's position; he acted as the moderator. When either man was ready to walk away from the conference, Carter kept them there by suggesting different approaches. He never gave up. If Sadat and Begin wouldn't talk to each other they could at least communicate through him. Clearly, it was Carter's determination that kept the talks going.

A peace treaty was finally formulated with each country compromising on certain issues. Israel agreed to withdraw from the Sinai Peninsula and to return the area to Egyptian control, while Egypt agreed to restrict the number of troops it would have in that area and guaranteed Israel's vessels safe passage through the Suez Canal and the Straits of Tiran. A second document was formulated in which they laid down the principles for future negotiations that would discuss Palestinian autonomy and the future of the Gaza Strip.

President Carter, with Sadat and Begin watching from a balcony, briefed a joint session of Congress on the Camp David Summit results on September 18, 1978. He received twenty-five minutes of applause. "Blessed are the peacemakers so they shall be the children of God," said an emotional President Carter.[8] On March 26, 1979, President Carter hosted a signing ceremony for the Egypt-Israeli peace treaty before a thousand assembled guests in front of the White House.

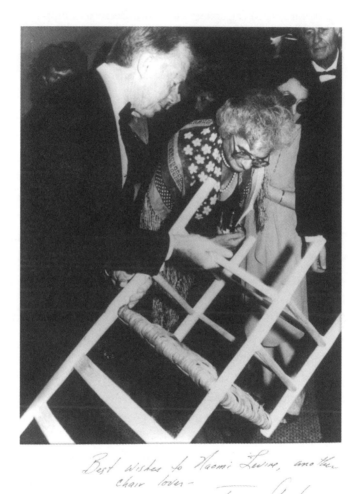

President Jimmy Carter and I. "Best wishes to Naomi Levine, another chair lover," reads the charming note Carter wrote at the bottom of the photograph. At an event we attended together, we discovered that we both had a love of beautiful, old, caned chairs (the chairs at Greylock were similarly fabulous).

While I had left the AJC the year before, I was invited to attend the ceremony. It was a thrilling moment in my life to be present at the signing of a treaty that meant so much to the security of Israel and hopefully peace in the Middle East. As we all know, it didn't work. Unfortunately, as the years moved on, Arab hostility toward Israel continued and there were many skirmishes and wars that followed. But, clearly the Camp David agreement was Carter's most important presidential achievement and established him as a global statesman. He was a man of hard work, honesty, ethics, integrity, and determination. "There will never be a history of the Middle East written without Jimmy Carter's name in the index," noted historian Douglas Brinkley.[9]

Even so, as I have already mentioned, the situation in Iran was to be Carter's downfall. In 1979, Ayatollah Ruhollah Khomeini became the new ruler of Iran. He set up a new government in that country based on the laws of Islam. At that time, the former Shah of Iran Mohammad Reza Pahlavi was exiled from his country following a revolution in which Khomeini became the ruler. The Shah came to the United States. Ayatollah Khomeini demanded that the Shah be released from the United States and sent back to Iran. Shah Pahlavi had been granted asylum in the United States for medical treatment for his cancer. The United States would not return the Shah to Iran.

As a result, on November 4, 1979, a group of Iranian students took sixty-six American citizens as hostages in the American Embassy in Tehran. Six Americans escaped and fled to the Canadian embassy. Thirteen more, who were women and Black people, were released later in November and many months later another hostage was let go due to illness. That left forty-six hostages still in captivity. For a year and a half, Iranian leadership kept demanding that the Shah be returned to Iran and the United States refused. All during this time, the hostages continued to be held in captivity. Every night Americans saw on their televisions the hostages blindfolded and exhibited to crowds in Iran.

The American public was furious. How dare another country treat American citizens this way? Why could President Carter not seem to do anything to correct it? Carter *was* trying. He tried a military approach, but that didn't work. He then moved quickly to apply diplomacy and economic pressure on Iran. The US stopped importing oil from Iran. Some Iranian nationals were expelled and billions of dollars of Iranian assets in the United States were frozen so Iranian companies could not do business.

Day after day, Carter kept negotiating. After 444 days, he finally got an agreement to get the hostages home. It occurred a day before Ronald Reagan's inauguration, giving the impression that the Reagan administration had arranged this agreement, but this was not true. Carter negotiated this deal. The deal consisted of the return of the hostages, while Iran got nine million dollars of their own money that had been frozen in US bank accounts since the crisis began. Carter worked on the agreement diligently between Ronald Reagan's election and inauguration, but unfortunately even this did not restore his reputation, as everyone believed that Reagan was responsible for the victory.

In addition to the Iran Hostage Crisis, the increasingly disastrous shortage in gasoline. sent his approval rating to 25 percent—a very, very low rating. The country had no faith in Carter or his administration.

In July 1979, Carter invited various business owners, labor leaders, teachers, governors, and mayors to Camp David to get their opinion on what he should do to turn the economy around. He went on television to tell the American public he invited these different people to help him find some sort of solution to the crisis. He talked again and again about conserving energy. He said, "First of all, we must face the truth, and then we can change our course. We simply must have faith in each other, faith in our ability to govern ourselves, and faith in the future of this nation. Restoring that faith and that confidence to America is now the most important task we face. It is a true challenge of this generation of Americans."[10] He asked his cabinet to resign. He brought in new people and new ideas, but whatever he submitted to Congress was not adopted. He had no friends among Congressional leaders and no one in Congress came forward to help him. It was an incredibly dispiriting moment in American history.

chapter seven

A Personal Tsunami

—★—

The election of 1980 showed how negatively the electorate felt about President Carter. He didn't connect with the people or with the Congress. Americans were deeply upset with him not just because of the Iran Contra crisis, but because of the economy. They were tired of his lectures about energy conservation, they liked their gas guzzling cars, they liked the new electrical appliances in their homes even if they used too much gas, and they were not interested in solar panels and other new technological ways of saving energy that Carter suggested.

Ronald Reagan was the opposite of Carter. He played poker and loved to gossip with his political friends and opponents. He was charming; he was a "people person;" he was a movie star; he was charismatic; he was tough on dissidents; he was a great communicator; and the people loved him. Indeed, when he left office in 1989, he had one of the highest approval ratings of all time.

The truth is there are many issues on which Carter was smarter than Reagan, but, nonetheless, Reagan and George H.

W. Bush, his vice president, had won the presidency. They promised to increase defense spending, cut taxes, limit the growth of the federal government, and ban abortion. They blamed all the problems in our country on the Democrats' liberal approach to government. They, of course, cited Carter's failures the hostage crisis and the bad economy. Reagan won 51 percent of the popular vote and 483 of the electoral college votes, while Carter received 41 percent of the popular vote and just 49 electoral college votes.

The Republican Party also gained seats in the House of Representatives and thus had their first majority in the House since 1952. On January 20, 1981, Reagan was sworn in as the fortieth president of the United States. This was just two weeks before his seventieth birthday. At the time, he was the oldest man in the history of the United States to assume that office.

Unlike Carter, Reagan's relationships with the Congressional leaders were very good. He was friendly, eager to please, and "a Hollywood star" whose glamour surrounded him. Nobody criticized him for spending $8 million on his inauguration. Nobody criticized Mrs. Reagan for spending $25,000 for a dress that she wore at one of the inauguration parties. The fact that Mrs. Carter bought her clothes off the racks in normal stores did not make the public like Carter any better. This is a dramatic example of how our country can be enamored with glamour and forget substance. I say this because Mrs. Carter, Rosalynn, was a terrific woman—smart, knowledgeable about current affairs, a strong supporter of her husband's goals. An expert on Latin America, she sat in on cabinet meetings. She was President Carter's closest adviser. Still, no one seemed to care about having such a brilliant first lady.

The newly minted Reagan administration made the economy the primary focus of its efforts. President Reagan's economic plan, called Reaganomics, was based on supply side economics. This approach to the economy involved cutting taxes on the wealthy and on corporations based on the theory that they would spend more money. More money would be in circulation, businesses would be able to hire more people, and ultimately the poor would benefit from more jobs and cheaper goods. Reagan's plan also included major cuts in government spending, but Social Security and Medicare were spared. The Omnibus Budget Reconciliation Act of 1981 reduced the budgets of 212 federal programs including food stamps, student loans, mass transit, and child nutrition programs. How the country could like Reagan in view of the cuts he made on these programs remains a mystery to me. The Economic Recovery Tax Act of 1981 also included reductions to personal income and business taxes, as well as reductions in capital gains, inheritance, and gift taxes (all of these helped the rich—and, in my opinion, pretty much no one else).

Reagan's plan did not help the economy right away. In August 1981 the US entered a recession that would continue throughout the year and get worse in 1982. While Reagan cut back on social programs and the needs of the poor, at the same time he called for expanded military programs and supported a build-up of the military. But the American public liked him anyway.

On March 31, 1981, nine weeks after his inauguration, as he left the Washington Hilton Hotel, Reagan was shot by George John Hinkley Jr., a drifter. Reagan's press secretary, a secret service officer, and a police officer were also shot. Hinkley, who was of course arrested, was found not guilty by reason of insanity and was admitted to a hospital for the mentally ill. Reagan, in spite of the fact that the bullet had collapsed one of his lungs, joked throughout the ordeal. "Honey, I forgot to duck!" he famously quipped to his wife in the hospital. How could you not like a man who said that after an assassination attempt? The public loved him more. It took several months for him to recover, but he appeared to bounce back quickly.

Early on in Reagan's presidency, 13,000 members of the Professional Air Traffic Controllers Organization (PATCO) went on strike. Because the organization's members were federal employees, it was illegal for them to do this. Reagan ordered the employees to return to work within forty-eight hours or lose their jobs. When they didn't return within that time period, new people were hired, and the striking members were fired. This destroyed PATCO, which went bankrupt, but Reagan's strong stance against the strike helped him establish an image as a tough and strong leader of the country. The fact that he destroyed a union was irrelevant, or so it seemed to the public at large.

But the most important cultural and political change that occurred during this period, without a doubt, was the end of the Soviet Union. Since the 1950s there had been a long decline in the rate of economic growth in the Soviet Union. Technologically, the Soviet Union was not keeping up with other countries. Its influence in foreign affairs was growing weak. Mikhail Gorbachev became general secretary of the Communist Party in 1985. To address what he saw as a crisis in his country, he instituted a program called Perestroika, which was the restructuring of the political and economic systems. On the political front, he legalized political parties other than the Communist Party. In 1989, Gorbachev established a Congress of People's Deputies that allowed contested elections and dissenting views. That Congress elected him the country's first president in 1990. On the economic front, Gorbachev permitted privately owned businesses and modified the system by which the Communist Party planned the economy. Gorbachev also put in place a policy of Glasnost, or openness, which increased freedom of expression. Soviet citizens were at once allowed to speak freely. They could read books such as George Orwell's *1984* that were critical of communism and had long been banned in Communist countries.

As usual, the more freedom people have, the more they want. He had hoped only to loosen the hold of the Communist Party on the life of the Soviet Union and the Eastern Bloc, not to do away with it altogether. The Eastern Bloc nations, however, were ready for more radical change.

The fifteen republics that made up the Soviet Union began to clamor for their own independence. These included the Balkan states of Lithuania, Estonia, and Latvia. By the end of the year, during Reagan's presidency, all of the Soviet Republics were pressing for independence. Gorbachev tried to meet their demands, offering a new treaty that would have given most Republics more independence.

But not everyone wanted the treaty to succeed. In August 1991, before the treaty could be signed, a group of hardline Communist party officials staged a coup against Gorbachev and his treaty. They were determined to stop his reforms and the loss of Soviet power. Gorbachev and his family were put under house arrest, but the coup did not succeed. It was defeated by thousands of Russian citizens who protested against it. The primary Soviet Republic, Russia, and its president, Boris Yeltsin, led the protest.

After the failed coup, the Soviet Union's days were numbered. Gorbachev retained little power. By November, thirteen of the fifteen republics declared their independence. In December of that year Yeltsin and the leaders of Belarus and the Ukraine, two of the Soviet republics, declared that the Soviet Union no longer existed. They announced that they were forming a loose association of former Soviet republics called the Commonwealth of Independent States and they invited other republics to join.

On December 25, 1991, Gorbachev resigned as Soviet president and the Soviet Union ceased to exist. In a period of two years, from 1989 to 1991, Communism had ended in Eastern Europe and the Soviet Union had faded away. This was truly a remarkable moment in history.

What happened in the Soviet Union inspired people in other countries in Eastern Europe to call for an end to Communism and to cut their ties with the Soviet Union. The countries in Eastern Europe wanted free speech, free elections, and an economic system that was better than that offered by Communist rule. With the Soviet Union being disbanded, many countries in Eastern Europe overthrew Communist rule between 1989 and 1990. They included Hungary, Poland, Czechoslovakia, Romania, Bulgaria, Yugoslavia, and East Germany. By the end of 1990, free elections were held in these countries resulting in non-Communist regimes.

Back in the US, two tragedies defined 1980s. One left a horrible image imprinted on the minds of a generation, and one changed the face of our society forever. The first tragedy I would like to discuss was that on January 28, 1986, the United States Space Program suffered the worst accident in its history when the space shuttle, *Challenger*, exploded just over seventy-three seconds after liftoff from Florida's Cape Canaveral. The entire crew perished in the explosion, which was viewed by millions of people worldwide on television. On board were commander Francis "Dick" Scobee, pilot Mike Smith, mission specialists Judith Resnik, Ron McNair and Ellison Onizuka, and payload specialists Christa McAuliffe and Greg Jarvis. The launch had originally been scheduled for January 22 but was delayed due to bad weather. The president appointed an independent thirteen-member commission that included former astronaut Neil Armstrong and Nobel Prize–winning physicist Richard Feynman and was chaired by former Secretary of State William P. Rogers to investigate this tragedy.

The Rogers Commission issued its report on June 6 which explained that the explosion was caused by a failure of rubber O-rings, which sealed the joints between sections of the solid rocket boosters and expanded as temperatures increased during the launch. In this case the O-rings failed to expand, allowing hot gases to leak, which in turn ignited the liquid fuel tank. A freak cold spell in Florida was partly to blame for the O-ring failure. At least two engineers from Morton Thiokol Inc., the company that manufactured the boosters, had voiced concern that at thirty-six degrees Fahrenheit the climate was too cold for the launch. The engineers apparently had also repeatedly advised senior management that the O-rings were problematic. NASA and Thiokol spoke prior to the launch, with NASA deferring to Thiokol's decision. Fearing that they would lose their business with NASA, Thiokol let the launch go on as planned. The conclusion of Reagan's touching tribute to the crew became perhaps one of the best-known quotes: "We will never forget them, nor the last time we saw them, this morning, as they prepared for their journey and waved goodbye and 'slipped the surly bonds of earth' to 'touch the face of God.'"[1]

On March 9, 1986, a Coast Guard ship found the bodies of all the astronauts still inside the intact crew compartment.

The second, and more lasting tragedy that defined a generation, was the AIDS crisis. In August 1983, Congress's Committee on Intergovernmental Relations and Human Services held hearings for more money for research to combat AIDS. Despite this, the Centers for Disease Control's requests for more money were denied. However, just two weeks after the hearings the budget was raised. A research team had determined that a virus caused AIDS. This was the first step to developing a cure. Since so many Americans had already died from AIDS, this was an important step forward.

President Reagan, however, showed little interest in the AIDS epidemic in the early years of his presidency. Only when his friend, the movie star Rock Hudson, contracted AIDS, did the president show his first interest in the disease.

This was a terrible time, with young men dying everywhere. There was much discrimination against AIDS patients, as the disease was associated with homosexuality. In Broward County, Florida any government employee who was diagnosed with AIDS was fired. Finally, on October 5, 1985, the day that Rock Hudson died of the disease, the House of Representatives doubled the funds for AIDS research to $189 million. The Senate raised AIDS funding to a total of $221 million. A breakthrough came in the fall of 1986, when medical research proved that the drug Azidothymidine slowed the progress of the AIDS virus. While the disease was still killing a large number of people, there was hope that this new drug would help in stemming the tide of this epidemic.

Because AIDS was such a real crisis in this country, the Surgeon General, Edward Coop, distributed 107 million copies of a booklet called *Understanding AIDS* as part of an education campaign against the disease. This didn't satisfy those who wanted the government to provide more research money so that there would be a faster approval process regarding different drugs related to AIDS. So, in October of 1988, 1000 protesters shut down the FDA Headquarters, demanding a speedier drug approval process for AIDS-related drugs.[2] In New York City and San Francisco, needle exchange programs were started in an effort to avoid the spread of AIDS contracted using dirty needles. Congress unfortunately did not fund needle exchange programs so no financing for these important programs was allocated.

President Reagan, as I have said, did not do as much as he could have about this terrible epidemic. He and Mrs. Reagan had another concern. They were both deeply troubled about the illegal drug use that was growing in this country. People who were drug addicts were also often involved in violent crimes. In August 1986, Reagan introduced a number of initiatives to reduce drug use. The President and Mrs. Reagan also launched the "Just Say No" campaign in an effort to deter young people from using drugs. President Reagan asked Congress for $900 million to be earmarked for the war on drugs. Congress was more generous and passed a plan that doubled Reagan's funding initiative.

Trying to reach drug users to prevent them from using drugs is an important approach But, the drug program announced by Reagan fell short on this component. The next Congress, I am pleased to report, gave more money for education and efforts to prevent people from using drugs.

Regardless of how good or bad the economy was, or how good or bad our foreign policy issues were, Reagan continued to be a very well-liked president. He had charm and an actor's ability to communicate. In 1984, when he ran for a second term as president, he was very popular. This popularity lasted even though during Reagan's second term, when more than 25,000 businesses failed. In that time, interest rates on homes and cars rose as well. In addition, the number of business bankruptcies and farm foreclosures rose to levels not seen since the Great Depression of the 1930s. Congress approved a tax increase of $98.3 billion in August 1982. This made Americans very unhappy. They elected twenty-six Democrats into seats held by Republicans in the 1982 midterm elections, but they still voted for Reagan as president in 1984.

Reagan, as a good Republican, also supported deregulation. Deregulation adversely affected the policies of the Environmental Protection Agency, the Food and Drug Administration, the Department of Transportation, and the Department of the Interior. As part of his deregulation plans, Reagan signed a bill allowing savings and loan institutions to "expand their market as it had been defined by federal regulations."[3] The deregulation allowed savings and loan institutions to offer higher rates and they made much riskier investments with their customers' money. Deregulation also allowed the Secretary of the Interior to offer the Pacific Coastline to oil companies for drilling. James Watt, the Secretary of the Interior, opposed environmental regulation. Public outcry over Watt's policies led to his resignation in 1983.

There is no doubt that Reagan moved the country in the direction of a more socially conservative phase. In 1988, family planning centers that received federal funding were forbidden to discuss abortion with their patients. In that same year, a man named Randall Terry founded Operation Rescue, an organization that blocked access to women's clinics where abortions were performed. And, to my amazement, the Supreme Court, in *Bowen v.*

Kendrick, supported a decision that denied federal funding to pro-choice programs. How do you reconcile this with *Roe v. Wade*? I do not know.

As Reagan's second term was coming to a close, Vice President George H. W. Bush ran for the presidency. The Democrats nominated Governor Michael Dukakis of Massachusetts. The Bush campaign attacked Dukakis for a soft position on crime. Bush promised not to raise taxes. "Read my lips: No new taxes" was the famous line from his campaign.[4]

In accepting the GOP nomination, Bush spoke of a "kinder, gentler nation."[5] He also stressed the importance of volunteerism and called volunteers "a thousand points of light."[6] Bush won the election, receiving 53.4 percent of the popular vote and 426 electoral college votes while Dukakis received 45.6 percent of the popular vote and 111 electoral college votes. A Libertarian by the name of Ron Paul ran in the election, too, and received 5 percent of the popular vote. Voter turnout was the lowest it had been since 1942. A sad sign for democracy.

Still, while the Democrats lost the presidency, they gained one seat in the Senate and two seats in the House giving them control of both chambers. This had not occurred since 1960. President Bush would now have to contend with fifty-five Democrats and forty-five Republicans in the Senate and 260 Democrats and 170 Republicans in the House. It was a tough Congress for him to do business with.

On January 11, 1989, Ronald Reagan, always the movie star, made a dramatic last television address from the White House in which he stressed that he was leaving the country, he believed, in very good shape. He was still enormously popular. His popularity rate was higher than any president had received since the time the polls were introduced in 1930.

Regardless of what he said, Reagan was not a great president, and the years during his presidency were not great. Some years were good, and some were bad. Unemployment was the lowest since 1974, but the federal deficit, defense spending, and the national debt increased dramatically. The rich got richer from tax cuts, while the poor got poorer. It was reported that women and children suffered the most as many social programs that had helped them were dropped. I certainly wouldn't give him more than a *B*.

Overall, the economy that he left to his successor, George H. W. Bush was not a good one, but it was improving. By 1989, the employment rate, 5.3 percent, was the lowest it had been since 1975 and inflation was stable at 4.4 percent. Fifteen million new jobs became available over the course of Reagan's presidency. The wealthiest 1 percent of Americans possessed 15 percent of the national income, an increase from 8.1 percent at the beginning of the decade. This gap between the rich and the poor, which continues today, was not a healthy development for our country.

It's hard for me to tell as I read through records of Bush's presidency what he did to make the country kinder and gentler, as he had promised. When Congress passed a minimum wage bill that would have increased the minimum wage from $3.35 per hour to $4.55 per hour, he vetoed the bill and Congress failed to override the veto. In November of 1989, a compromise was reached to raise the minimum wage from $3.35 to $4.25 over the course of two years.

Bush did make an effort to improve the public schools. He felt that more could be done with the money they had. He advocated rewarding schools that showed improvement with underprivileged children. His educational programs provided pay incentives for teachers, and he brought together at a summit on education the governors of all the states where it was agreed that national performance standards should be established.

He also continued Reagan's war on drugs. On September 5, 1989, he announced a $7.9 billion plan in which half would go to law enforcement programs involving drugs and, in 1999, under his direction, Congress passed an $8.8 billion allocation adding

$900 million for treatment and educational programs to Bush's initial proposal.

During Bush's presidency, the Supreme Court handed down a decision that burning the American flag was protected by the First Amendment and was a form of freedom of speech. Bush was very unhappy with this decision. He sought a constitutional amendment that would protect the flag. The Speaker of the House, Thomas Foley, offered the Flag Protection Act of 1989, which was passed by the Senate, but the new law was ruled unconstitutional by a federal judge. When it was appealed to the Supreme Court, it was again declared unconstitutional. The proposed amendment that was supported by Bush was defeated by both the House and Senate in June 1990.

The Supreme Court handed down another decision of great importance during Bush's presidency. In July 1989, in the case of *Webster v. the Reproduction Health Services of Missouri*, the Supreme Court ruled that states could impose restrictions on abortion. The religious right was unhappy since the court did not overturn or reverse *Roe v. Wade*. Bush announced his support for an amendment banning abortion. Congress, on the other hand, submitted legislation designed to loosen the federal restrictions on abortion, but all were vetoed by the president. It's interesting to note that a quarter of the forty-three bills that Bush vetoed were abortion related. In my mind, there was nothing kind or gentle about his approach to abortion which kept so many women from making the choice whether or not to have a child.

During George H. W. Bush's presidency, Congress also slashed the budget for the National Endowment for the Arts. There were people in the Congress who felt that some of the art exhibited was too sexy, referring to the work of the great photographer Robert Mapplethorpe, which was sexual, sadomasochistic, and homoerotic in nature. But art is meant to challenge society, not to comfort it. I do not believe that Bush made any effort to stop this.

As I noted, during his campaign, President Bush repeat-edly said that he would not raise taxes on the American people. After becoming president in 1989, George H. W. Bush kept his promise of no new taxes until November 1990, when he broke that promise. In that year, he signed legislation that increased federal taxes because the national debt had grown so heavy in the Reagan years. By 1990, the federal budget deficit was $220 billion, three times what it had been a decade before. So, in spite of his campaign promise, Bush was forced to raise taxes to reduce that enormous budget deficit that Reagan had built up. Obviously, the polls then showed that Bush's popularity dropped precipitously for breaking this pledge. To make matters worse, the economy was going badly.

Then came the war in Iraq. The first one, I mean. In 1990, Iraq, led by its president Saddam Hussein, invaded Kuwait. Kuwait is a very small country, but it is oil rich. Hussein claimed that Kuwait was part of Iraq. He argued, moreover, that Kuwait was producing too much oil, which caused oil prices to decline. It took six days for Iraq to eliminate any resistance that little Kuwait could offer. Kuwait became part of Iraq.

The day of the invasion by Iraq, the United Nations issued a resolution condemning the attack. The United States was a major part of that international force opposed to Saddam Hussein. Thirty-nine countries were part of the coalition. They included the United Kingdom, France, Germany, Spain, Eastern European nations such as Poland and Czechoslovakia, and Arab countries such as Egypt, Saudi Arabia, and Syria. On November 29, 1990, the United Nations passed a resolution saying that unless Iraq left Kuwait by January 15, 1991, the Security Council approved all necessary force to achieve that goal. In other words, if Iraq did not leave Kuwait by January 15, 1991, the coalition would declare war.

By the time the deadline arrived, Iraq still occupied Kuwait. At that time there were 700,000 coalition troops in the region, including 500,000 US troops. They were supplied by a great many

US tanks, warships, combat aircraft, and some very sophisticated technological military equipment provided by the United States. The coalition launched aircraft bombings wherever Iraqi troops were installed and then they waged a ground assault. Iraq did not have the troops or the sophisticated military equipment to sustain its defenses. Just four days after the start of the coalition's ground war, about 100 hours, the coalition "ended its military operations." Iraq's army had been driven out of Kuwait and decisively defeated. Kuwait was liberated. On April 6, 1991, Iraq formally accepted a ceasefire agreement.

The Persian Gulf War gave Americans a good feeling in that it dispelled the ghosts of Vietnam. The Gulf War made it clear that in certain circumstances the United States would be prepared to go to war and could defeat a powerful enemy with few casualties.

—

As for me, I joined New York University as senior vice president in 1978. When I came to NYU, the university was close to bankruptcy. It owed $40 million. The philanthropy team was raising for the whole university, including its hospital, medical center, and law school, approximately $20–$30 million a year. The university had funds sufficient for only three months operation, and the clerical staff and faculty were asked to voluntarily take a cut in their salaries.

Competition from other universities was severe, especially after City University announced open enrollment. Academic standards at NYU were modest. Fundraising was not very impressive. The school had few, if any, dorms. It was a commuter school with most of the students taking the subway to school every day and living at home. NYU was not a university of "first choice" for students or faculty. During the 1980s and 1990s, we changed NYU's standards, its academic image, its fundraising strategy, and its physical landscape of the surrounding Greenwich Village and the East Village.

Today, just forty years later, NYU is not only financially stable but recognized as one of the world's most acclaimed centers of education and research. It raises more than $500 million a year and is currently completing one of the largest, if not the largest, building campaigns of the last decade, which included the building of six new dorms, a sports center and scores of labs and classrooms. How did this happen? What kind of miracle achieved this? Of course, it was not a miracle. It was based on a very specific approach to fundraising that became a priority for the university.

Before I arrived, when the university was struggling to survive, the board brought in John Sawhill as the new president. He was not an academic. He had worked in the business world and had a PhD from NYU Stern. His career had been in both corporate financial services and management and in government as the director of the Federal Energy Administration. The university thought his experience outside of academia might be useful in whipping the institution into shape.

The first thing he did of course was try to balance the budget. He was relentless in cutting costs, avoiding duplication academically and administratively, and consolidating departments where necessary. Still, despite the wrenching cost cutting and the firing of scores of people, the financial health of the university remained precarious. It became clear to Sawhill that the only way to save the university was through fundraising.

Until that time, fundraising efforts at NYU were minimal. Indeed, the chairman of the NYU Board of Trustees was John Schiff, a very famous financier in New York City. He believed that boards should not raise money and that raising money was a crass use of a board. John Sawhill was able to remove John Schiff as chairman of the board and brought in Larry Tisch. Mr. Tisch's attitude toward the role of a board in fundraising was the opposite of that of Mr. Schiff. Larry believed that boards must play a critical role in the fundraising of a university or any nonprofit.

He believed that boards should run according to the three Gs: board members should **Give** financial support, help **Get** financial support, or **Get** off the board. You do not sit on a board for your ego. You sit on it to help keep the organization which you are committed to alive.

The formidable Larry Tisch and I at a formal event.

With George H. Heyman, Jr., one of the best men I've known.

Mr. Tisch with his brother Robert, owned Loews Corporation which comprised hotels, real estate, insurance, and Lorillard tobacco, among other business ventures. Most important, he was very well liked by other businessmen. He believed that major gifts would come from a group he called FIRE: finance, insurance, and real estate. So, he put on our board the most important people from those sectors of industry. He appointed George Heyman from Lehman Brothers the chairman of the development committee to work most closely with me. From the world of finance, he also brought in Ace Greenberg from Bear Stearns and Bill Berkeley, a banker from Greenwich, Connecticut. From real estate, he brought in Larry Silverstein, Lewis Rudin, Bob Tisch, and Leonard Stern. From insurance, he had John Creeden from Metropolitan Life and Maurice Greenberg from AIG. It was one of the most powerful boards in New York City and that was key to our fundraising success. Larry Tisch, John Sawhill, George Heyman and I then developed the rules that we would follow in our fundraising efforts. Below are just a few of the most important ones.

1. The first rule was a very simple one. Fundraising must be viewed as an obligation of the whole organization and not something that can be done only by a fundraising staff.
2. The whole university, including the president, the chairman, the board, the deans, and the faculty, were to be involved if NYU was to survive. I repeat: fundraising cannot be left only to a development staff.
3. The role of the president, the board, and its chairman, as I said above, is critical.
4. A development office must be viewed as an important component of the university. It must be respected by the whole university. It must have on it people who are smart, interesting, verbal, and deeply committed to the mission of the university. They are to be well paid and respected by the entire university.

It is important to keep in mind that development people must be interesting human beings. They have to be able to write and speak and relate to people. Fundraising requires developing relationships. You cannot develop relationships with a donor if you are not able to talk with him or her about the issues of the donor's interest or issues of communal concern. You don't meet with a donor and just ask for money. That may be part of it, but it is not all. The cultivation of people is at the heart. Here is where the art, not the science, comes in. Here is where your personality and how you relate to people are key. By adulthood, much of a person's personality is set, but there are ways to change it. Read magazines on development and fundraising, but more importantly read *The New York Times*, *The Economist*, *The New Yorker*, and other magazines. Read books and join an organization. Become a whole person. Be interested in the society in which you live. Show that you are interested in current issues in politics, education, health care, the environment, women's rights. This makes it possible to cultivate a donor by discussing areas of her interest. When Larry was involved with CBS, I asked the development staff that was in touch with him to read everything the press was reporting about CBS.

5. Staff must understand why people make gifts. Instead of buying a yacht, why should someone give money to an organization or charity?

6. And, lastly, most important to me, a development person must know the state and federal laws that govern fundraising so that the decisions he or she makes are ethical and legal.

So, these were the main principals we developed. And we had the full support of Sawhill. Indeed, to send a message to the entire community about the importance of the development staff, Sawhill moved my office next to his and met with me and my staff several times a week.

For me, meeting the important and successful people who were involved in my fundraising made my job especially exciting. Still, these were not easy men to work with. You could not waste their time. You had to be well prepared and talk succinctly, making your requests very clear. I used to spend a great deal of time preparing for any phone call that I was to make to any of my board members. While I was often the lone woman in the room, never in my twenty years in working with the board did I ever find that they treated me improperly because of my gender. That was never an issue that entered our relationships.

Given the importance of these extraordinary individuals in my life, I would like to dedicate a few words to some of our board members, those who were particularly influential. I believe their characters help explain why and how fundraising at NYU became so successful.

First: Larry Silverstein. Larry bought the Twin Towers a few months before 9/11. It was his practice to have breakfast every morning with one of the major tenants in the building. The morning of 9/11 he had a breakfast set in the restaurant on top of one of the towers. As he was getting ready to leave the house for that breakfast, his wife Klara reminded him that he had a doctor's appointment. She urged him to change his breakfast meeting and go to the doctor. Larry argued with her, but Klara won. So, Larry went to the doctor instead of going to breakfast. He is living today because of that decision and because Klara was the winner of that argument. Larry tells this story with great emotion since it is a case where his wife's direction saved his life.

Larry was one of the most dedicated members of our board, a wonderful donor and human being. Everyone liked Larry. He may well have been a different kind of person in business, but as a member of the board, he was very helpful, not only making his own gifts but helping Larry Tisch and me meet other men and women in real estate. He was always a joy to work with and never once made me feel my gender was a deterrent. He respected his wife, Klara, very much. She was a real partner with him in his business. And making him go to the doctor that morning saved his life.

Larry Silverstein and me.

Another important member of our board was Arthur Balfour. Arthur was also a major philanthropist in our country. At a very young age, he was a feather salesman in Poland. Every morning he would go out with his satchel of feathers to try and sell them to make a living. At three o'clock, he would call his wife and ask her if she needed anything. One day, she said, "Don't come home. The Nazis are close to the village. Go through the woods to our family and hide for a while." Arthur's family was killed by the Nazis who stormed into his village, killing his wife and children. Arthur spent the next year in the woods, hiding out. Finally, after doing this for a year, he accumulated enough money to buy one ticket to come to America. When he came to the US, his relatives met him at the boat. They helped him get a room and also a job selling candles door to door before he got a job in a feather company where the owner spoke Yiddish. Every payday, Arthur took half of his money and bought feathers and stored them in a garage. His friend asked why he was buying feathers rather than new clothes or shoes. Arthur said that he knew the United States would soon enter the war and he knew they would need sleeping bags which needed feathers. He was right on both counts. The United States entered World War II and our government then called for companies that would bid on the government contract for sleeping bags. Arthur had bought the feathers at a low cost, so he got the contract. Then, he went back to New York and hired a group of women refugees and rented sewing machines. The result: every soldier in the US Army carried a sleeping bag made by Arthur Balfour.

I could go on with story upon story about these men, but I think these two tales will give you some idea of why I found these people so fascinating. I should stress that they not only were successful and interesting businessmen, but they were also deeply committed to NYU and other areas of philanthropy. I have said many times that the university would not be here today without their dedication. It was their hard work that enabled us to raise $2.5 billion in twenty-five years and that saved the university.

But it was not always roses, of course. Sometimes the work was difficult. Dodo Bobst was the only trustee of NYU that I ever had any trouble with during my twenty-five years at the NYU. I was in Florida and had a luncheon date with Dodo Bobst, whose husband, Elmer, had given NYU a major grant for our Bobst Library. The Bobst Library is the centerpiece of the university and literally changed the face of NYU. It created one of the great open stack libraries in the country and gave the students of NYU a beautiful building on Washington Square in which to study and enjoy the thousands of books at their disposal. During my stay in Palm Beach, I made a date with Dodo Bobst for lunch to discuss a gift that she might give to the library. On the morning of that luncheon, she called me to say that she had set the luncheon up for Dr. Brademas, then the president, herself, and me at the Everglades Club, but unfortunately the club did not accept Jews even for lunch. She asked if I would mind if they had lunch without me and then she and I could have another lunch some other time and some other place. I was shocked. I could not believe this. I spoke to Dr. Brademas and, of course, he did not go with her for lunch that day. I told him from then on, I would prefer that he handled any university relationships with the Bobsts. He agreed and I never spoke with Dodo again in the years that followed. To this day, I cannot believe that an educated woman would not understand how embarrassing it was to tell me I couldn't eat in a certain restaurant because I was Jewish. Who would believe that such discrimination still existed in this country.

But, for every one of these negative interactions, I can think of a thousand positive ones. For example, it was my great honor to work closely with John Loeb, who was the chairman of the board at the Institute of Fine Arts and came from one of the most distinguished families of the city of New York. I once set a meeting with John for a luncheon at the Four Seasons, a restaurant that Mr. Loeb preferred. During those years, I suffered from small fibroids in my uterus that would bleed on different occasions. I ultimately needed to have them taken out, but at this time I was still suffering from this condition. When the bleeding occurred, I usually went to the doctor or the hospital. I had no way of knowing when the bleeding would begin.

During my lunch I went to the bathroom and, to my dismay, discovered I was bleeding. I was very embarrassed to have to discuss this with a man I hardly knew, but I had no option. I came back to the table and told John the truth: I was bleeding and I had to get to the doctor. He told me that he was a trustee of Mount Sinai and that his car downstairs would take me there at once. He got me in the car, took me to Mount Sinai, got me a room, got a doctor immediately, and within twenty-four hours I was treated and able to go home. He couldn't have been nicer or more helpful. He stayed at my bedside until Leonard and my parents arrived.

Over the years John and I would have lunch at the same table at the Four Seasons every month or so. We enjoyed talking with each other about all the problems of the world. It was his custom after our lunch to walk me to my car and see that I was seated comfortably for my ride home. On the last visit I had with John, I saw that under the table he had placed a walker. He had obviously had a fall or an operation. When we finished lunch he asked me, "Do you mind, Naomi, if I don't walk you to your car? I hurt my leg and it pains me to walk." I told him that of course I understood. He managed to get up and hug me before we said goodbye. We both had a feeling that this would be the last time we saw each other, so the goodbyes held a particularly poignant feeling, for me, at least. We hugged and he walked me as far as he could with his walker. He then asked one of the waiters to walk me to my car. And, of course, he slipped that waiter a generous tip. I must say, as an aside, they don't make men like John Loeb anymore. I don't know how to explain this, but he was a particular kind of old-fashioned gentleman, a wonderful philanthropist, a great friend to me and to NYU. I often think of him and miss the kind of approach to life, to philanthropy, and to women that John knew. To me, he was very special.

———

But while my work life was in full swing, something happened, something I never could have anticipated. In the middle of the 1980s, 1985 to be exact, I was hit by a personal tsunami. I was 67 years old. His name, for the sake of this story, was Charlie. Charlie was one of the most successful and important lawyers in the South

Florida area—covering Palm Beach, south to Miami and north to Jupiter. His main law office was in West Palm Beach where he had a law firm of at least 25 lawyers, with five partners. They had a small outpost of five lawyers in Miami. Charlie was affluent, a philanthropist, and well known in political circles in the area.

NYU Law School was interested in having Charlie on its board and asked me to see if this was possible. By luck, I found out that Charlie was a friend of Roger Lewis. Roger arranged a dinner for Leonard and me (Leonard often joined me in Palm Beach), Charlie and his wife Eleanor, and Roger and his wife. We ate at a fancy restaurant. It turned out to be a very pleasant dinner with Charlie, Leonard and me all agreeing that the Republican administration in the local area was terrible. Roger and his wife were relatively silent, since I think they are Republicans and were ashamed to admit it.

Charlie went to Columbia Law School two years ahead of me. He had been a soldier in the war and was a GI veteran. He was relatively good looking, with gray hair, piercing blue eyes, and a great smile. He was tall, trim, and he exercised at the gym every day and was very careful with his diet. He loved telling me I kept him off the moot court committee at law school because his grades were not that great. I had no recollection of this, but that did not stop Charlie from telling the story twice. He narrated it with humor and no hostility.

Most of all, it was clear that Charlie was a chatterbox, and that he had a great sense of humor. Eleanor was very pale, quiet, and coughed a great deal. I was told it was rare that she came out for dinner. She was recuperating from a lung operation. Our dinner went on for well over three hours. It was a fun evening, and for me it was the beginning of a new relationship.

But I still had not talked to Charlie about NYU. I was not sure how to proceed. Thank goodness, Charlie took the next step. His law firm was holding a lecture as part of a series they sponsored, on charitable lead trusts, and he thought I might be interested in coming. I jumped at the chance, although my interest in charitable lead trusts was zero.

Charlie's office was impressive, with lots of pictures of him with important people on the walls. The three partners I met seemed like very nice men, especially Andrew who seemed to run the firm, and the lecture was not quite as boring as I expected. The buffet at the end was terrific and worth my being bored. I still did not know how to make my approach about NYU. There were at least fifty people present, and Charlie was busy talking to each of them. But, eventually, to my delight, Charlie came to my rescue.

"Was it boring for you?" he asked.

"Not too bad," I answered honestly.

"How about lunch sometime so I can show you I know a great deal about charitable lead trusts, and I can make it exciting. You might even put me on the moot court committee."

We both laughed.

"Of course, Charlie," I said. "Any day next week, except Friday. I am leaving for New York on Friday."

We had lunch on Tuesday. Charlie was great to be with. We talked a lot and laughed more. Finally, I got my nerve up. I told him about NYU Law School. He said that he had heard that it was now one of the best.

"Would you like to be on the board?" I asked.

"Well," said Charlie, "I turn down these requests all the time. I don't have the energy. I am 67 years old. But in this case, I might say 'yes,' if it would give me the chance of seeing you some more— maybe in New York and in Florida. So, the answer is 'yes.' What will it cost me?"

I was taken aback by his answer. I never expected it. It usually took at least three luncheons to get a reply. And this was so personal, as well as so fast. Charlie later told me that I turned red and stumbled in my response.

"No, no. No money, just your brains," I said, which I knew was a lie.

"You're lying, Naomi. But yes, I'll serve on the board, and, in the future, I'll talk about money."

I could not believe my luck. We finished lunch and I thanked him. We made another lunch date for Thursday, and I left for New York on Friday.

When I got to New York, there were flowers waiting for me from Charlie with a card. "Will you let me be on the moot court committee?" the note read. Throughout the next five months, which I spent in New York, there were lots of notes from Charlie and lots of notes in return from me. Best of all, Charlie joined the NYU Law School Board. They were having a trustee meeting at the Breakers in August, and he attended. The dean was delighted. I was busy in New York and could not attend. Charlie was a little amazed at this, but he reported he enjoyed the board meeting and met some interesting lawyers and judges. He and the dean got along very well, and I was sure a gift would come soon. My job was done. I thought my relationship with Charlie was now finished.

How wrong I was.

I did not hear from Charlie for several weeks until September, when I heard from Andrew, his senior partner in his office, that Eleanor had been very sick during these months. She had many operations and had died of lung cancer. How cruel to die so young. She was about sixty years old.

On the phone, Andrew said to me, "Charlie is busy with the funeral and family matters but wanted you to know he thinks about you."

In July, Leonard had a heart valve operation. It went very well. We spent a quiet August and September as he recuperated. By September, we were able to go to the Adirondacks and spend ten days at Greylock. The leaves that turn red and yellow and gold in the Adirondacks in the fall make the mountains look like a picture postcard. But Leonard did not want to make the trip to Florida. He did not feel up to it. So, in November I went alone.

I called Charlie when I got to Florida. We made lots of dates—lunches, dinners, Kravis Center shows, galas in support of some charity, and lectures that Charlie's firm and other organizations gave. The truth is, I enjoyed being with Charlie regardless of what we were doing. We talked endlessly. We laughed, we gossiped, and, of course, we shared stories about our families. I returned to New York in May.

I came back to Florida in January with Leonard. He was feeling better. My brother, David, and one of his new girlfriends joined us (by this time, he and Helen were divorced). While we were there, Rusty Gulden, a real estate broker told us about one of her clients who had a two-bedroom apartment at Sun and Surf, one of the loveliest building complexes in Palm Beach. Naturally, me with my interest in real estate and no money, I asked her to introduce me to the lady. Suffice it to say, I got a tremendous deal. David, Leonard and I, bought the apartment. Between the three of us we managed to get the money for the down payment. A mortgage did the rest.

Having an apartment in Palm Beach made more sense than having to stay at the Breakers, which cost me a great deal of money and cost NYU a great deal of money when I was there on business. Because of our new apartment, Leonard and I stayed an extra week while David and his friend went back to Washington. During this time, I invited Charlie to join us for a meal. He did so but seemed uncomfortable. So, I did not press him. When Leonard went home, I stayed on for another week of appointments with donors.

With Leonard gone, Charlie and I resumed our dates nearly every other day for lunch, dinner. One day Charlie said to me: "I want you to see a place that I have that I run away to when I want to be away from the tensions of the world." "I would love to see it," I replied. He then drove me about a half or three-quarters of an hour outside of Palm Beach to a place I think was Fort Lauderdale on the water and showed me the place that he "ran away to." It was a magnificent yacht. I have seen some very beautiful yachts. Larry Silverstein has one of the largest and most beautiful. Charlie's yacht was stunning. Maybe it was because the sun was shining brilliantly on it. Or, maybe it was the excitement and pleasure that shone in Charlie's eyes when he showed me the boat.

I boarded the boat and got a tour. It had three magnificent state rooms, lovely living and dining rooms, and several decks. There was one deck on which you could eat informally, and it gave you the feeling that you were eating on the water. There was a large crew, including the captain of the boat and his assistants, a chef and assistant chef, and many other staff that I could not identify. Charlie and I had a magnificent lunch on the boat and talked and talked.

"So, you think it is nice?" Charlie asked.

"Not nice, Charlie," I said. "It's stunning."

We then retired to the living room to relax. I never saw Charlie so at ease. We talked mostly about Eleanor's last days.

"It was awful. She had several terrible operations and was always in pain," he told me.

"You know, Charlie, I do not want to be kept alive at such a point," I said.

"Seeing her in agony, neither do I," he replied.

And so, we chatted, drank some wine, and left the boat by 4 p.m. Charlie had an appointment and so did I.

Thus, my boat life with Charlie began. From then on, all our meals were on the boat. One day, Charlie suggested he take the boat to the Cayman Islands. There was gambling there, and he loved to gamble. We arrived in the Cayman Islands at 6 p.m., ate a great dinner, and Charlie then went to the tables. I don't gamble, so all I did was watch Charlie lose thousands of dollars at the poker table, the dice table, and the slot machines. It was not his night, but he confessed to me that he always lost but enjoyed it anyway. The fact that he lost so much money did not disturb him at all. I looked on in awe. How could he be so calm when he was losing so much?

By 9:30 p.m., I told him I had had enough and wanted to go home. He good naturedly agreed, and we returned to the boat. It had started to rain and, by the time we were out on the water, a real storm with thunder and lightning broke out. I was scared to death. I am scared of boats in sunshine, so imagine how I react in storms. The boat was big, but it rocked dangerously with blasts of thunder and high winds. The waves were high. I could see them from the window in my state room. I was petrified, sure that the boat would go down and that I would drown any moment. Charlie joined me, trying to convince me that all was well, and this yacht could handle a storm. I was not convinced. He held me close and, before I knew what happened, friends became lovers.

The next week was a jumble in my mind. I saw Charlie sometimes twice a day. He wanted me to divorce Leonard and move to Palm Beach. I couldn't leave my NYU vice presidency. I loved my work, and I would not ask Charlie to leave his job. (There is a gender difference here that I won't bother to discuss.) Moreover, I was not going to leave Leonard at that point. He was not well, and I was not going to divorce him at that stage of his life.

I was caught. I realized that I loved Charlie—a new emotion for me. There was no question: I wanted to be with him. I enjoyed him. I talked more with him that I did with most people. I laughed with him. I know he felt the same way. On the boat, we just enjoyed the peace and quiet, reading and making love. How could I feel this way? This was teenage stuff, not the emotion of a 67-year-old lady. Yet it was how I felt.

But, still, I remained firm, I could not divorce Leonard. I could not leave New York. The most I could do was to come to Florida more often, which I did. For the next few years, I spent from October through May in Florida and, even during the summer, I would take a plane down to Florida for a weekend. I always made up a good excuse for why I had to go. Frankly, I do not think that Leonard suspected anything.

At the same time, Charlie came to New York and Washington

where he had some business. It was the best we could do. Actually, we were spending a good deal of time together and enjoying every minute of it. In New York, I made the plans and I think we saw every show on Broadway. We went to every museum and ate at every restaurant. I was happy and so, I believe, was Charlie.

During this period, though, a great tragedy occurred in my life. In 1997, David and several members of the State Department went to the city of Tbilisi in the Republic of Georgia to help that country design their constitution. He called me on a Saturday night and told me they were successful, they had finished their work, and he would be coming home on Sunday night. He asked if he could stay in my apartment in New York City before returning to Washington. I, of course, agreed.

David deep in thought in a meeting.

—

The next morning at 9 a.m. I got a call from the American Embassy in the Republic of Georgia telling me that my brother David had been killed in a car accident. Apparently, after he had finished working on the constitution, he and his aide had done some sightseeing, alongside a couple of translators. They drove as tourists to see a very beautiful church on a hill outside the city of Tbilisi. On the way down from the church, they were hit by a truck and all of them were killed, except for David's aide who was badly injured and airlifted to a hospital in Israel. I was in shock, and to this day, so many years after that accident, I find it hard to even write about it. I was unable to deal with the situation, so my daughter Joan called the State Department, was patched into the American Embassy in the Republic of Georgia, and made the arrangements for the return of David's body. Two days later, at 4 a.m., the American Embassy in the Republic of Georgia called Joan to say that they would not release David's body unless the family agreed not to "press charges" thereby making an international scene. Joan told the Embassy that such a decision had to be made by David's children, not by her. His children, now adults, made the decision to have his body returned. David's body was returned: naked, with no passport or any information or clothing.

My daughter and nephew believe this was a deliberate murder as several people in Georgia opposed the United States interference in their drafting of Georgia's constitution. I had no desire to pursue this, and the family respected my wishes and let the issue go. In the middle of the city of Tbilisi, there is a beautiful new library, and it is named in honor of my brother. I could not go to the dedication, but David's son Jeffrey went and is very proud of the remarks that were made about David by officials of the government of Georgia.

Below is a quote from a letter from Al Gore, at the time vice president in the Clinton administration, to David's daughter,

Elizabeth, on David's death—an example of how people in the government in the US and The Republic of Georgia felt about David. The letter was read at his memorial service. I keep a framed copy of the letter in my apartment in New York City and at Greylock.

> From 1994 your father served with distinction in Russia, the Ukraine, Georgia, and other new independent states helping those states establish the rule of law. He worked with judicial leaders, nurturing the development of legal cultures in countries where democracy and free markets were just starting to take hold. In leading these key assistant efforts on behalf of our nation, he was an American pioneer.
>
> At an early stage of his career your father showed unique promise in winning the Arthur S. Flemming Award given annually to ten outstanding young people in the US government. Three decades later he was still serving his country with notable dedication in often difficult circumstances. As the rule of law developed in the new independent states, David's contributions remained a living gift to future generations.

These words touched us greatly as a family, but my grief for David was profound. I missed him, and I kept learning about him after his death. At the memorials for David in Washington, DC, and in New York City, women came and introduced themselves and told me of their warm relationships with him. They all found him charming and enjoyed whatever time they had with him.

Of course, this was after his relationship with Helen had ended. Helen was twenty and David was twenty-five when they were married. Both their mothers thought they were too young to marry, and time proved them correct. In 1970, they were divorced, but not before they became the parents of Jeffrey and Elizabeth.

While the children lived with their mother following the divorce, David remained a devoted father and both children spent nearly every weekend with him and most of their summers with David at his house at Camp Greylock. He bought the house from Leonard and me when we closed the camp.

Our entire family spent (and continues to spend) the summers together at Greylock. It became a very special place in our lives. David's children became very much a part of my family and Joan and her children became part of theirs. Greylock kept us together. Helen also remained very much a part of our family and spent her summers with us.

All I can say about David is that I guess every life is a novel in its own way. If I were Tolstoy I could do a much better job about David's life, but unfortunately, I am not. My brother led an extraordinary life, made many contributions to the pursuits of democracy in Latin America and in Europe, and his family is very proud of his memory.

So, in that period, I was mourning David, but I was comforted by my warm, loving relationship with Charlie. Still, life is cruel. Nothing good lasts forever. One day in 1999, I received a phone call from Andrew in Charlie's office. Charlie was in the hospital; he had had a heart attack. He was feeling better, the doctors told him he would be going home soon. I called Charlie at once, planning to get to Florida that night.

"No," said Charlie, "I should be home by the weekend (it was a Tuesday). My family and my daughters and brother and sister-in-law and two aunts and cousins are here day and night. If they saw how I looked at you, they would understand our relationship and my daughters would be shocked."

I agreed that we could wait until Friday. I got tickets for a plane to Florida. On Friday morning Andrew called. Charlie had died. I could not believe it. I got the call at work. I went from the office to the ladies' room, and in a private toilet I cried myself sick. I am not a crier. But this was different. I could not stop. I managed to walk the three blocks from my office in the NYU Bobst Library to my home. I cannot explain how I felt. All I could think was: *How can I live without him?* More tears . . . My world came apart.

Andrew called again. His voice showed that he was as upset as I was.

"He told me to bring him his blue suit to go home in," Andrew said. "'I have a big date Friday night,' Charlie told me."

I cried some more.

Andrew continued, "When I came to the hospital, he seemed in a good mood. He was shaving. He put his pants on and then asked me to help him to his bed. Then he said, 'I suddenly feel very tired.' He took my hand. He looked funny. I helped him onto the bed. He kept holding my hand and closed his eyes. I yelled for the nurses. They rushed in. Doctors came. He had had a second heart attack and died at once. I could not believe it." Andrew stopped. His voice trembled.

I could not talk. Finally, I broke the silence. "Why don't you call later," I said.

"Yes. The funeral is next Sunday, and a memorial will be at the office a week from today. Are you coming?" he asked.

"No," I answered.

Thus ended the call that changed my life and brought me a grief I would never get over.

The next few days were misery for me. But as usual, work was my medicine. I was very busy, and I was able, thank God, to concentrate on that. It was September. We were planning a trustee retreat at the Breakers in February. I had to start planning now. I also had to return to Florida by October—something I dreaded. Time moved quickly, though, and by the time I stopped crying, it was the end of October, and I returned to Florida alone. Leonard could not go with me. It was as terrible as I feared. No Charlie waving and smiling at the airport. I had ordered a car beforehand and went directly home.

After Charlie's death, it seemed to me that the rest of my life would be but a footnote. I went on with my fundraising for NYU. To my amazement, my performance continued to be very strong. I received many accolades and awards—but they all meant very little to me.

Leonard was also beginning to show signs of the illnesses that would later contribute to his death, but by and large he was able to go to work part time and go with me to Westport on the weekends. I spent much of those years caring for Leonard as a quasi-nurse. In the end, he was confined to the bed. I tried very hard to be at home as best I could to be with him to make up for all the years I was never at home.

Before long, Leonard was tormented by illness. First, he had operations involving his throat, and then the doctors found a growth on the pancreas. They initially thought it was pancreatic cancer, a deadly disease. After operating, they found it was not a cancerous growth. Instead, it was a benign tumor, but he was never the same after that operation. He developed an infection in the biliary duct that caused him to spike high fevers at unexpected times even when he was home, so frequently I had to rush him back to the hospital. And then, he did ultimately develop pancreatic cancer.

By that time, Leonard was worn out, physically exhausted, and mentally very depressed. Since I still had to go to work sometimes, I hired a nurse to be at home with him all the time in case he spiked a dangerous fever.

One Saturday night, my best friend Betty held a party in Westport in honor of Leonard and me returning from Florida. Since Leonard was not capable of driving to Westport, we took a car first to Helen's house and then we planned to drive up to Westport with Helen and her husband, Dr. Sidney Horowitz.

When Leonard and I arrived at Helen's house at 25 West 81st Street, I entered the building first. The door was very heavy and swung back and hit Leonard in the head. He fell. Helen and

Sidney came down at once. Leonard said he felt fine. Dr. Horowitz checked him and agreed that he was okay, so we went to the party. We got there around 9 p.m., and at 10 p.m. Leonard said he felt "very tired" and wanted to go home. That was very unusual for him. He loved Betty's parties and liked to stay and socialize as long as possible, but we went home on his request. Overnight, he had a massive brain hemorrhage caused by the swinging door. He never woke up. He died on February 18, 2001.

Leonard and I were married for fifty-five years. While our relationship was often strained, his death left me unhinged. In many ways, he was my anchor. We were very different people, but we supported each other in very important ways.

I loved people, but Leonard was happy just to be alone with me. I was ambitious, but he was content with a modest job as an accountant in a large accounting firm. I was prepared to fly high, and he was content to walk safely on the ground. But, oddly enough, we needed each other, and we each added to each other's lives.

We were very young when we married. He had just come out of the army and would have married any woman who would have accepted him. He was twenty-seven and I was twenty-five. I was under great pressure from my mother and aunts who thought that marriage was the next important step I should take. If I didn't get married soon, I would become an "old maid," a state that no Jewish woman should allow herself to enter. Leonard and I, therefore, did not think seriously about the kind of person we should marry.

Over the years, we had many disagreements, mostly about Camp Greylock, but at the same time we were indispensable to each other in the more than half century of our lives which we shared.

Leonard and me in our later years.

On September 10, 2001, I went to bed early, as my NYU colleague Ann Marcus and I had a breakfast meeting with Florence Davis of the Starr Foundation at 8 a.m. on September 11 at 70 Pine Street, the headquarters of Starr.

Our breakfast began promptly at 8 a.m. We saw the second plane hit the World Trade Center tower and saw people and desks fly out the windows. In retrospect, we did not know what we were seeing. I sat in shock by the window. Ann grabbed my hand and dragged me to the elevator, and we got out—on the last elevator working in the area (electricity was cut off after the attack). Police instructed us to walk north. Ann and I joined the march of people streaming uptown.

I could not get over how kind people were. They helped each other. Storekeepers offered us free water. Others offered sneakers to ladies with high heels. A young man offered to carry my attaché case. After about five minutes on the march, we heard a loud terrifying noise. We looked back as the tower collapsed and the whole area around it was engulfed in black smoke. If Ann had not gotten me out when she did, I think I would have died of that smoke. I owe her my life. Whenever she wants something from me, she reminds me of this in good humor.

After about an hour, I made it to Bobst Library. How I did that long, long walk I do not know. But I made it. When I came into my office all my staff was there and applauded my safe arrival. I collapsed in my chair, delighted to be "home" and to be with my colleagues who looked genuinely happy that I was alive.

On the march north, Ann and I saw scores of people running south crying. They had loved ones, friends and family caught in the tower. There were almost 3,000 people who died in the tower. These people, crying and running south, did not know whether their loved ones were alive or dead. You can be sure they were assuming the worst. Some police who were rushed to the scene tried to keep them from going south. I could not see the confrontation, but we later learned that many such confrontations took place. All we heard on that march was what sounded like a group crying.

As I marched, I thought of Charlie. What would he have to say about all of this? My tears for Charlie were a trickle in the storm of tears that fell that day. I will never think of Charlie without thinking of 9/11. And I will never think of 9/11 without crying for Charlie. It was a tragic moment in American history and, of course, a tragic time in my life. On that march, history and I became one.

chapter eight

I Knew It Was Almost Over

Reagan's shadow fell all over the years that followed his two-term presidency. It was Reagan's Doctrine that the presidents of the 1990s, Bush and Clinton, carried forth. It was Reaganomics that formed the basis of the approach to economic theory throughout the entire decade. The longest economic boom in the nation's history that the 1990s enjoyed had its beginnings in the 1980s. And the enormous deficit that Reagan left played an important role in Bush's and Clinton's budgets. Reagan, as a devoted Republican, believed in small government, a strong military, and low taxes. These policies, too, had a great influence in the decade that followed.

In the 1992 election, President George H.W. Bush was the Republican nominee for president. His Democratic opponent was Bill Clinton, who had been the governor of Arkansas. Clinton was not well known and had not been an especially impressive governor. He was 45 years old, very youthful and charming, and had the ability to connect with people on every level. Bush was

67 years old, much more reserved, and was often accused of being an elitist from a very wealthy family that did not understand the average American.

Clinton won. He received 370 electoral votes to Bush's 168. On the popular vote, Clinton won 43 million votes to Bush's 39 million, with a third-party candidate, Ross Perot, receiving 20 million. Clinton had won only 43 percent of all the votes cast—not even a majority of the votes. This suggested the country was severely divided.

During the campaign, Clinton made it clear that his priority was getting people jobs. James Carville, who was a strategist on Clinton's campaign, coined the phrase "It's the economy, stupid," which was often repeated that election cycle. Clinton was also concerned about the very large federal deficit that Reagan and Bush left.

As soon as he entered office, it was clear that he was going to have a difficult time getting his programs adopted. The Democrats were divided, and the Republicans made no qualms about the fact that they were hostile to him. Indeed, Newt Gingrich, who was the Republican minority whip, made it clear that he disliked Clinton very much and he would block any program that Clinton pushed.

The media, too (for reasons that I do not understand), was constantly looking for bad things to say about Clinton. They talked about the fact that in Arkansas he was known as a womanizer, that as a young man he smoked marijuana, and that he did not fight in the Vietnam War. Conservative talk radio hosts such as Rush Limbaugh lampooned and criticized Clinton from every angle. Conservative magazines such as the *American Spectator* attacked him openly. He was ridiculed as "Slick Willy," someone given to lies. When a Clinton aide, Vince Foster, committed suicide in 1993, rumors, which were never substantiated, spread through the anti-Clinton media that Clinton had him murdered.[1]

There were other instances where the Republicans took every opportunity to give him trouble. It was discovered that his nominee for attorney general, Zoe Baird, had hired household help for whom she neglected to pay social security taxes. A storm of controversy broke out and the nomination was withdrawn. The next candidate, Kimber Wood, had the same issue, and her nomination was also withdrawn. Finally, Janet Reno was nominated and approved, becoming the first female attorney general, but the Clinton administration was embarrassed.

It also caused a great deal of controversy when Clinton tried to make it possible for gays to serve openly in the military. Military and Congressional leaders resisted, so Clinton finally backed down and accepted a compromise policy on homosexuals called "Don't Ask, Don't Tell." The compromise satisfied very few people and left Clinton looking weak on military matters.

Another one of Clinton's actions that caused a great deal of controversy was when he appointed his wife, Hillary, to head a committee to develop a plan for health care reform. In Arkansas and in Washington, DC, Hillary was not liked. During the 2016 presidential campaign, when she ran for president against Donald Trump, many people voted for Trump because "they didn't like her." I never could figure this out. I knew her personally. I found her to be wonderfully charming, very intelligent, a brilliant lawyer, and someone with a great sense of humor. But apparently, her political persona was not winning, and there was something about her that turned people off. She was not a good campaigner. I do not know what made her unpopular. Maybe the public was not ready to accept a very brilliant woman as a political partner with her husband. Maybe she was too smart, and perhaps the public does not like women who are too smart. I do not know what it was that made the public dislike her, but whatever it was, I found it deeply disheartening. She had to live up to the marvelous ways in which her husband was able to connect with voters.

Nonetheless, Hillary Clinton became a part of her husband's administration. During the beginning of the Clinton administration, Hillary developed a sweeping plan for universal healthcare reform that would cover all Americans. Many in Congress, including Democrats, thought it was too complicated, and the insurance agencies and business leaders opposed it. In 1993, President Clinton sent the plan to Congress. They rejected it.

Scandal did seem to follow the Clintons wherever they went. Clinton was also charged with financial misconduct concerning the Whitewater Development Corporation. This corporation had bought land in Arkansas for vacation home development, and the Clintons had invested in this company from 1978 to 1982. Later, the company was alleged to have done some unethical acts. Both Clintons denied wrongdoing, and his administration appointed an independent council to conduct an inquiry into this issue. In August 1994, a panel of federal judges appointed a Republican lawyer, Kenneth Starr, to lead the Whitewater Investigation.

As I noted before, one of Clinton's most forceful opponents was Newt Gingrich, a Republican Congressman from Georgia. Gingrich outlined certain conservative goals that he was going to achieve on behalf of his Republican colleagues. They included balancing the budget, fighting crime, restricting spending, strengthening national defense, and placing term limits on legislators. In the midterm elections in 1994, the campaign for these goals was a success. Republicans won control of the Senate and gained a majority in the House for the first time in forty years. In January 1995, Gingrich was named Speaker of the House. He continued to make life for Clinton a constant struggle.

There was another incident that added to Clinton's difficulties. In 1995, he and the Republicans in Congress fought over the budget. Both Republicans and Democrats wanted to get rid of the deficit, but the Republicans wanted to do that by cutting spending for programs that Clinton thought were necessary for the average American. Clinton thought the Republicans' suggested cuts were too sharp, and he presented his own plans. The

Republicans rejected those plans. They could not reach an agreement. In October 1995, the government failed to pass a budget, and so it shut down.

Many government operations ceased for a period that lasted from November 1995 through January 1996. Hundreds of thousands of federal workers were sent home and government services were disrupted. Each side blamed the other, but the polls showed that Clinton came out looking better than his Republican adversaries. Republicans expected him to be weak enough to give in. He did not. He stood firm and projected an image of strength by refusing to back down from his principles. By 1996, the budget issue was settled, much to the satisfaction of Clinton. The government shut down was over.

Clinton was also able to push reform of the federal welfare program. Many liberals felt the program was not generous enough to the poor, while conservatives thought it was too generous. Clinton's bill placed limits on how long welfare recipients could keep receiving their aid, but most importantly it shifted much of the responsibility of running the program from the federal government to the states. This was very controversial. Many in Clinton's own party were very distressed and believed that it hurt the poor. Clinton felt that his bill was a compromise. The Republicans had submitted bills that were harsher than Clinton's.

Clinton was lucky on one count. Throughout his presidency, the United States enjoyed a very healthy economy. It was the longest economic boom in the nation's history. There were new jobs, higher wages, and new industries that developed around the Internet, cell phones, personal computers, and information technology. China, India, Singapore and, with the fall of the Soviet Union, new markets in Eastern Europe opened for US business. Under Communism these countries had high barriers against trade, capitalism, or free markets. Now the barriers were gone. All of this helped immeasurably in building the economy and keeping the boom going.

Some of the things that the Clinton administration did also helped in creating and sustaining this boom. Each year, Clinton paid off a part of the deficit that Reagan and Bush had established. This was an important contribution to the economic strength of the country.

The wealthy, as in every economic boom, benefited the most. The rich were much more likely than other people to own a significant amount of stock and so they profited disproportionately from the booming stock market. Many middle-class Americans were intrigued by the stories they heard about how much money people in the stock market were making. They bought stocks, not checking on whether the stock represented companies that were really doing well. And when the stock market frenzy collapsed, as all booming stock markets eventually do, many of these people lost a good portion of their money. The gap between the poor and the rich grew wider, as it has continued to do. I found this very troubling at the time (and still do). I believe this gap poses a significant threat to the stability of our country.

In the same vein, the Clinton era also saw a wave of downsizing, as companies tried to become more productive by reducing the number of employees. Many large companies laid off workers or moved their operations overseas. Obviously, employees in such circumstances lost their jobs. Some found work in the service sector of the economy which included restaurants, hotels, clearance stores, etc., but these jobs did not pay as well and did not provide good benefits. But, overall, most of the jobs that were developed offered good salaries and good benefits.

In 1996, Clinton ran for reelection. Many people liked him and respected him for defending his budget during the government shut down. The economy was doing well, and his popularity was high.

Senator Bob Dole challenged him as the Republican nominee for president. Dole was a World War II war hero and was a Congressional leader for many years. He was a difficult opponent for Clinton. But Clinton had achieved much, in spite of all the difficulties he faced, during his first term, including job creation and the lowest rates of unemployment, inflation, and interest in almost thirty years.[2] During the campaign, Clinton pointed out that he had indeed reduced the deficit, submitted bills that reformed welfare, increased the minimum wage, and offered a tax cut for fifteen million Americans. He noted that crime rates had fallen, and he was putting 100,000 more police officers on the streets. He had a very impressive record of achievement to build his campaign on. At the time, Dole was seventy-three years old, and Clinton was fifty. Clinton's youthfulness and his achievements were also very persuasive to voters. Bill Clinton had a special ability to connect with people, one of those critical attributes for politicians. We cannot forget his ability to connect with his phrase "I feel your pain."

Clinton won the election by an even bigger margin of electoral votes than he had in 1992, gaining 379 electoral votes to Dole's 159. Clinton was the first Democratic president to be elected to a second term since FDR in 1936.

Nonetheless, scandal continued to follow the Clinton presidency. Clinton's second term was marred by the incident involving Monica Lewinsky, a twenty-two-year-old intern at the White House with whom Clinton had sexual relations. Kenneth Starr, the independent council no longer restricted to only exploring the Whitewater charges, began to investigate if the president lied under oath when he said he did not have sexual relations with Lewinsky. He was also interested in whether Clinton had encouraged Lewinsky to lie in her testimony, thereby obstructing justice. Clinton continued to deny these charges, but eventually he admitted to a grand jury that he had "inappropriate intimate contact" with Lewinsky and, later that night, confessed the same thing publicly in a televised address to the nation. While he admitted to misleading people, he insisted he had not lied under oath.

On September 9, 1998, Starr sent a report to the House of Representatives outlining possible impeachable offenses arising from the Lewinsky scandal; two days later, the document became public. Starr's report found that Clinton had not been truthful when he testified in front of the grand jury and had encouraged others to do the same. All around the globe, people read the nitty-gritties of the president's affair.

So, in December 1998, the House passed two articles of impeachment against Clinton. One accused him of perjury and the other charged him with obstruction of justice. The House passed the first article by a vote of 228 to 206 and the second by 221 to 212. The Senate, however, found him not guilty of the first count by a vote of 55 to 45. They voted 50 to 50 to find him not guilty of obstruction of justice. Clinton had been acquitted of both charges. All of the Democrats and several Republicans had voted to acquit him.

As with the Iran Hostage Crisis for Carter, the Lewinsky scandal followed Clinton. No positive action he took as president is as remembered as much as his bad judgment during that period.

———

Before I move on to my life during this period, I do want to pause to discuss one of the most horrific events of the decade, which occurred at the end of the '90s. We are living with its effects still. On April 20, 1999, two students at Columbine High School in Jefferson County, near Littleton, Colorado killed fifteen people in their school, including themselves. All throughout the '80s and '90s, there had been an alarming increase in school violence, but Columbine was the worst to date. Americans tried to understand what happened. Was it violent video games and violent movies that caused this? Others, like me, blamed the easy availability of guns. Whatever the cause, the issue of school violence became a major subject for communal discussion.

Unfortunately, there have been many other shootings at schools since Columbine. I must confess that I do not understand why this country cannot adopt a law that prohibits the sale of guns of the kind that these boys had at their disposal. Those guns were used in war, and they should not be in the hands of civilians. The argument that the Second Amendment prohibits us from passing such laws is, I believe, an incorrect interpretation of that amendment. Every effort to effectively control the sale and use of firearms since then has tragically proven unsuccessful.

———

As for me, during the 1990s, I continued to work closely with Larry Tisch and George Heyman to raise the funds we needed to keep the university growing. In 1994, NYU was given La Pietra in Florence, Italy, by the will of Sir Harold Acton, a British philanthropist. We rebuilt La Pietra into both a center for the European Studies Program that NYU developed in Europe and as dorms for students who were studying abroad. We raised a sufficient amount of money to make this development possible.

We also began to raise funds for expanding the work we were doing in computer science. We took over several buildings in Brooklyn where such programs were being developed and as the years moved on, we were proud to say how effective we were in this drive.

During this period, we also completed our first billion-dollar campaign; we were one of the first universities to complete such a campaign. My life was entirely tied up with these efforts. We had many luncheons, dinners, and special meetings with prospective donors.

One especially bright spot though, was that in 1996, Dr. Arthur Hertzberg and I were reunited as coworkers. We founded the Bronfman Center for Jewish Student Life at NYU and were able to get Edgar Bronfman to provide the funds necessary for the center.

My whole life at this point was relatively quiet. While I continued to raise money with Larry, George, and other members of the NYU family, I had already developed techniques that worked to do so, and I didn't find the pressures of my job overwhelming.

chapter nine

With the Terrible Donald Trump, I Have Not Been Able to Sleep

I began this book by writing about the period which brought my family from Europe to America. I will end with the year of 2020. This covers more than a hundred years—a century of history and a near-century of my own life.

The decade of the 2000s did not start off in a happy way. As I already mentioned, the century opened with the September 11 attacks when nearly 3,000 people were killed when the terrorists attacked the World Trade Center in New York City and the Pentagon in Washington, DC. These disasters announced the beginning of global terrorism, which unfortunately marked the opening years of the century. In addition to the attacks against the New York City World Trade Center, there were three other terrorist attacks that followed in quick succession. First, there was a terrorist attack in Madrid, Spain on March 11, 2004, when ten bombs exploded on four commuter trains killing 191 people and injuring 1,800. Second, on July 7, 2005, Al-Qaeda set off four bombs in the city of London, three in the subway and one on a bus in one of London's squares. Fifty-two people were killed and seven hundred injured. And third, on November 26, 2008, in Mumbai, India, ten men from a Pakistani terrorist organization went on a three-day shooting spree in hotels, restaurants, on the streets, etc., killing one-hundred-and-sixty-six people and injuring three hundred.

In addition to global terrorism, during these years we have also witnessed the devastating power of nature, as thousands have been killed by earthquakes and hurricanes. These natural disasters included a powerful earthquake in 2004 in the Asian Pacific area set off by a tsunami that killed hundreds of thousands of people. Then, in 2005, Hurricane Katrina swept into the Gulf Coast areas of the United States resulting in New Orleans being submerged under water, 1,833 people killed, and thousands left homeless along the Gulf Coast. And, in January 2010, another massive earthquake devastated Haiti, killing 230,000 people and leaving thousands more homeless.

These natural disasters underscore the fact that, although mankind through its technological advances has done much to give people a better and more secure life, nature is more powerful than man and can destroy what we have created. Can we survive? What can we do?

I don't know whether we can survive, but I do know that there are ways we can try to save our planet. Climate change should be discussed and addressed. It should be a top priority for all nations. If we do not have the earth, we have nothing.

So, the beginning of the new millennium was marked by terrorism and natural disasters. Not a good start. As a result of 9/11, President George W. Bush, announced that the United States was now at war with Afghanistan. "Tonight," he said, "we are a country awakened to danger and called to defend freedom. Our grief has turned to anger and anger to resolution. Whether we bring our enemies to justice or bring justice to our enemies, justice will be done."

And so, on October 7, 2001, the Bush administration invaded Afghanistan on the theory that that country harbored Osama bin Laden along with other leaders of the Taliban who played a role in the World Trade Center disaster. The war's purpose was to demolish the terrorist organization "and bring its leaders to justice."

Two years later, the Bush administration decided they saw a connection between Al-Qaeda and Saddam Hussein, the Iraqi president. On March 20, 2003, therefore, the United States went to war against Iraq, in addition to our ongoing war against Afghanistan. The goal was to destroy Hussein's reign and find "weapons of mass destruction" that the Bush administration felt existed in Iraq. After ten days of land and air battles, the weak Iraqi army gave up and the war technically ended. Chaos continued to plague Iraq and things went from bad to worse. In December 2003, Hussein was captured. Three years later he was tried and executed.

Still, there was a major bright spot during this decade of turmoil, and that was the election of President Barack Obama. Obama, elected in November 2008, became president after George W. Bush. President Obama was the first Black person to be elected president of the United States. Who can forget the sight of Jesse Jackson crying at Obama's acceptance speech in Chicago? Obama was by all accounts a very bright, committed, and decent man and was an effective president. He was re-elected for a second term in 2012.

Violence in the Middle East and Afghanistan seemed to have dropped dramatically by late 2007. With the conflict declining, President Barack Obama worked to bring the wars to an end. In February 2009, he declared that combat operations would cease in eighteen months. In August 2010, the president announced a reduction of troops in Iraq from 144,000 to below 50,000. No one is sure whether violence will come back to Iraq once US soldiers leave. Some experts say that the Iraqi central government is too weak to keep order. Others believe the United States could do little more for the fledgling democracy, so it's just as well that we are leaving.

At the present time, some American troops remain in Iraq as part of a UN force. They are there not to fight but to train Iraqi soldiers and to try and keep the peace that now exists there.

Afghanistan remained a violent and lawless country. According to Obama, Iraq was the wrong war. We should have concentrated on Afghanistan where bin Laden had planned the 9/11 attack. In his first year as president, Obama ordered a 17,000 troop increase to help calm this country and to keep Al-Qaeda from reorganizing there. The president's decision to raise troop levels was very controversial, as many Americans just wanted to get out of the war and concentrate on jobs and the economy.

Despite the Obama administration's emphasis on Afghanistan, the most pressing foreign policy issue was the impact of its neighbor, Pakistan, which is a nuclear armed nation. Evidence suggested that Pakistan was harboring Osama bin Laden and other terrorist masterminds.

On May 2, 2009, the Obama Administration acted on that evidence. That night US Navy Seals, a highly trained group of commandos, raided a residential compound in Abbottabad in Pakistan and shot and killed bin Laden. Hours later his body was buried at sea. Days later Al-Qaeda vowed revenge.

President Obama was responsible for many important pieces of legislation, including

- The Affordable Care Act (Obamacare)
- The Dodd-Frank Wall Street Reform Act
- The Consumer Protection Act
- Repeal of "Don't Ask, Don't Tell" Act
- The American Recovery and Investment Act of 2009
- The Tax Relief, Unemployment Insurance Reauthorization, and Job Creation Act
- Budget Control and the American Taxpayer Relief Act

Obama also urged the Supreme Court to strike down same-sex marriage bans as unconstitutional. Same-sex marriage was fully legalized in 2013. In addition, he advocated for gun control in response to the Sandy Hook Elementary School shooting, indicating support for a ban on assault weapons. He issued wide ranging executive actions concerning global warming and immigration. He was awarded the Nobel Peace Prize in 2009. Obama's presidency has generally been regarded favorably, and evaluations of his presidency among historians, political scientists, and the general public place him among the upper tier of American presidents.

I was in awe of Obama and saw his political success as a sign of great hope, but still, one turn of events has distressed me greatly in the last few years. I am thinking of the resurgence of anti-Semitism in this country and in Europe. It is very disturbing. Indeed, there has been a 70 percent increase in anti-Semitism in Europe and more than 30 percent in the US. As I write this book, *The New York Times* reports that there has been a noticeable increase in antisemitic activities in New York City. The police are now more focused on this issue, and the Jewish community is holding meeting after meeting to try and understand what is causing this and what they can do to try and alleviate the problem. At this point, I can offer no solutions. I view antisemitism today as a delusionary and irrational effort, and I'm not sure that any rational program can cope with it. I apologize for the negativity of this attitude, but unfortunately decades of experience inform it.

As for me, for a long while, my career marched. In 2001, I created the George H. Heyman, Jr. Center for Philanthropy and Fundraising at NYU. The center's purpose was to teach fundraisers and other people who have a responsibility to keep their organizations financially alive how to raise money. The Heyman Center gave courses on every aspect of fundraising and philanthropy, offering non-credit courses that led to a professional certificate as well as graduate courses for a master's degree. William Josephson, a lawyer and former Assistant Attorney General, and I gave the course on "The Law, Ethics, and Board Governance of Nonprofit Organizations." We taught that course for more than ten years.

Receiving the NYU Presidential Medal,
flanked by former NYU University Presidents
Dr. John Bardemas and Dr. L. Jay Oliva.

During this time, a very impressive gala was held in my honor on October 27, 2005, to raise funds for the Bronfman Center on Jewish Student Life. Nearly all the trustees attended, and we raised several million dollars. This pleased me very much. I received the NYU Presidential Medal, the highest award the university bestows, signed by three presidents and I also received an honorary degree from Hebrew University and a special honor from the NYU College of Nursing. All these achievements made me enormously proud.

However, in the early 2010s, I began spending an increasing amount of time in Florida, and Bill and I gave up teaching the course. Soon, the Heyman Center ceased to exist. Nonetheless, during its tenure, the Heyman Center was viewed as an important part of the world of philanthropy and fundraising.

Unfortunately, to bring us up to the present, I must now turn to a subject that grieves me greatly: Donald Trump. Trump was elected president in 2016. While Obama is viewed as one of the best presidents of the United States, Donald Trump is viewed by many, including me, as one of the worst. This is supported by many historians, political scientists, and psychiatrists and in many articles by reputable magazines and books.

Trump prides himself on the fact that he does not read and has very little patience with briefings. He has no regard for the Constitution or the laws that make up our nation. He says repeatedly that the Constitution gives him authority to do whatever he wants. He gets his information by watching Fox News and television generally.

His attitude toward immigrants is mean and nasty. He shows no compassion and no regard for the fact that we are a nation of immigrants. He has called the immigrants from Mexico "rapists," though he has given no evidence that Mexican immigrants are any more likely to commit the crime of rape. He has taken money that has been allocated to many other sources (especially to military projects) and threatens to use that money in order to build a wall to separate Mexico from the United States, so immigrants have no way of illegally entering this country. He has told American military servicemen to stop at his hotels whenever they are in the area so that the Trump organization can make additional money from this practice.

Three years after his election, on December 18, 2019, the Congress of the United States impeached President Trump.

President Trump was impeached on two charges:

1. Abuse of power
2. Obstruction of justice

Let us examine each of these further:

- **Abuse of power:** It was reported that he held back military aid to the Ukraine until its president agreed to dig up dirt about Vice President Joe Biden, whom he thought would be the Democratic opponent to him in the 2020 presidential election.
- **Obstruction of justice:** President Trump was accused of withholding important documents from the Congressional committee investigating the impeachment and not permitting certain people to testify.

Unfortunately, the Senate, which was majority Republican, acquitted him on both charges. He now struts across our TV screens saying that he has not been impeached. He says constantly that he did nothing wrong and has nothing to apologize for.

Trump went on to pardon eleven of his cronies. They were imprisoned for a variety of reasons, such as tax fraud, lying to Congress and other government officials, tampering with witnesses, failing to pay taxes, violating security laws, Medicare fraud, marijuana related charges, failing to report a felony in a bribery case, and other illegalities of that sort. And, if my mother was correct that you can judge a person by the friends they have, the picture you get of Donald Trump is not a happy one.

Many articles in respectable periodicals and new books all conclude that Trump is "unfit to be the president of the United States." Indeed, more than 19 books have been released recently, which are all dedicated solely to arguing that Trump should be removed from office.

Numerous articles arguing the same have also appeared in magazines such as *The New Yorker* and *The Atlantic* and daily papers such as *The New York Times* and *The Washington Post*.

Nonetheless, in 2020, Donald Trump decided to run for president again. He ran against Joe Biden, who had been the vice president under Barack Obama for eight years. During his campaign, Trump exhibited many signs of his psychological problems such as his narcissism and arrogance, and complete sense of entitlement. The question facing the public was this: does the president exhibit a consistent pattern of behavior that suggests he is incapable of properly discharging the duties of his office? Even Trump's own allies recognized the degree of his narcissism. When he launched racist attacks on four Congresswomen of color, Senator Lindsey Graham exclaimed, "That's just the way he is! It's more narcissism than anything else." He is a man, moreover, who seems to completely lack empathy, a terrible quality in a leader.

Indeed, when Trump thankfully lost the election to Biden, he behaved in a way that serves as a dramatic example of all of his sociopathic tendencies.

In the weeks leading up to the election, my friends and I had extensive discussions about which city or country we would go live in if Donald Trump were reelected president. After much debate, we chose London or Canada. Neither one was especially appealing, as London is very rainy, and Canada is very cold.

Happily, we do not have to make this decision. When Biden won the election, my friends and I were happy to say that we were unpacking our suitcases and could remain in New York City. Trump is not giving up, however. He refuses to recognize the election of Joe Biden. He claims that the election was fraudulent, rigged, as he puts it, and that he is being denied the presidency due to a deceitful and dishonest election. He has brought lawsuit after lawsuit, but I'm happy to report that all of the lawsuits he has brought to date, he has lost.

Let us hope that now the country may finally be free of Donald Trump. Like all the books that have been written about him, I believe that he has truly been "unfit to be president of the United States." Thankfully, the American public came to that same conclusion and voted for Biden.

—

And, yet, despite the years of the Trump presidency, as I reach the end of my life, I cannot help but think how much I have to be thankful for, my family, especially. I have a terrific daughter, Joan Kiddon, and I have two wonderful grandchildren, Chloé and Olivia. Joan is an extraordinary woman. She is a very private person, and this book is not about her. Suffice to say she has always been very attractive and very brilliant. Joan, together with her business partner, Larry Light, has written four books on branding. She and Larry have their own company, Arcature LLC, in Delray Beach, Florida.

My daughter Joan.

Chloé attended Stanford University and has a Ph.D. in artificial intelligence from University of Washington. She works at Google in a managerial position. She is married to Dr. Alex Salskov and they have one daughter, Elowen. (Chloé's and Alex's second daughter, Linnea Naomi, was born in May 2021, four months after Naomi's death in January 2021.) Olivia graduated from the University of Miami with a Bachelor of Fine Arts degree, specializing in art and photography. She fell in love with the restaurant business and is now a manager at an exceptional, popular, well-regarded restaurant in Miami Beach.

My granddaughter Chloe

My granddaughter Olivia

My nephew, Jeffrey Bronheim has lived in London for twenty years and is managing partner of the London office of Cohen & Gresser. He married Elvira Barroso. She is an independent scholar, who researches book history and the trade of heretic books in Iberia. She recently catalogued 2,111 documents for the Prize Paper Project in the National Archives in Kew. One of their children, Georgina, is an art student at the Rhode Island School of Design. And Samantha, their other daughter, is majoring in biology at the University of Manchester.

My niece Elizabeth is a partner at Sussman Shank, LLP, a law firm in Portland, Oregon. Her law practice focuses on helping employers navigate legal issues related to employment law including discrimination, harassment, and medical leave.[2] Her husband Harry works in sports television. He acts as a stage manager for broadcast events including for the Portland Trail Blazers, Timbers, Oregon Ducks and Beavers, and as a field producer for clients such as the NBA, MLB and other production studios.

Their daughter, Darcie, is a forestry major at Cal Poly in California and their son, Nate, is a student at the University of Oregon.

I want to say also a word about my special friend and family member, Helen Horowitz, who was married to my brother David for many years. During the last years of my life, Helen has become my closest friend and confidante. She is not only a friend, but a member of my family. But let me also add a note about our professional relationship.

The women in our family at Camp Greylock.

Helen worked with me briefly at the American Jewish Congress when she moved to New York with her children in the early '70s and later worked for me at NYU for many years as the director of media relations in our department of public affairs. Helen's team was responsible for making "news" of our campaign to thrust NYU into the first rank of American universities. She saw to it that NYU's name, its faculty, and its achievements were highlighted in articles in national newspapers, like *The New York Times* and the *Wall Street Journal*, on national and local television and through radio interviews. Indeed, our publicity campaign played a really valuable role in NYU's success: any mention of NYU in *The New York Times* virtually guaranteed a positive response from the donors for whom I was responsible. So, the work of the public affairs department was a top priority for all of us. Helen went on to similar roles at Fordham University and at the New York Botanical Garden, before retiring and turning her energy to volunteer work with low-income primary and secondary school students. Helen has played so many invaluable roles in my life, as an indispensable a colleague working with me at NYU, one of my best friends, and an important part of my family.

And, since my family were scattered all over the globe—London, Florida, Oregon, Washington, and New York—friends were very important in my life, too. As I close out this book, I'd like to say a few words about the friendships that have meant the most to me.

At the American Jewish Congress, I made some of my closest friends, who remained with me nearly all of my life: Will and Betty Maslow, Phil and Betty Baum, Lois Waldman, Betty and Mal Warshaw, and Rae Weiss. Betty was my best friend for many, many years until she died a few years ago. She not only was very smart but had a great sense of humor and there was not a serious issue that Betty and I could not laugh through. Betty took my place as director of the Women's Division when I moved on from that position. These were the friends who played poker with Leonard and me at Fire Island, spent weekends with us in Westport, and even schlepped six hours in a car to spend time with us at Greylock.

Three Executive Directors
Will Maslow 1960–1971
Naomi Levine 1971–1978
Phil Baum 1994–

Will Maslow, Phil Baum, and me, or, as the caption puts it
"Three Executive Directors."

Also, during my time running Greylock I made friends with several campers and counselors. This included Vincent and Walda Corazon. Vincent was head of the water program and helped make Greylock one of the great waterfront camps. There were also several campers, such as Janie Gaynor, Nancy Einstein, Laura Stein, Lynn Meadows, and many others who have continued to write to me, visit me, and call me and continue to be a very special part of my life.

When Leonard and I bought a house in Westport, we became very good friends with Herb and Mildred Abrams, Betty and Hank Corwin, and Jeanne and Leo (Budgie) Gordon. They made our time in Westport a delight.

When I came to NYU in September of 1978, Dr. L. Jay Oliva was the chancellor. He became later president from 1991 until May 2002. He was my dearest friend at the university. He had a complicated home life, and so he did not go out in the evenings. His friendship with me took place at lunchtime or in the afternoons. But it was a deep and meaningful one. I loved him dearly and I know he felt the same way about me.

With Dr. L Jay Oliva and Larry Tisch.

In my role at NYU, I worked very closely with Laurence Tisch, chairman of the NYU board of trustees. He was wonderful to collaborate with and his talents and connections were invaluable. The Chairman of the Trustee Development Committee was George Heyman, who also worked very closely with me. He was one of the smartest men I ever met. Larry and George put together a very impressive development committee that included: Larry and Klara Silverstein, Leonard Stern, Michael Steinhardt, Richard Bernstein, Preston Robert Tisch, Shelby White, and Geraldine Coles, and many others. They were indispensable in our fundraising drive which raised $2.5 billion in twenty years. They opened the doors to affluent donors, and they made major gifts themselves. I had lunch and dinner dates with each of them all the time and developed professional friendships. I enjoyed their company very much.

They were very different kinds of friends than those I had from the American Jewish Congress. They were all very affluent men and women, and I learned in my relationships with them that our society is severely divided economically. It was not appropriate for me, as much as I liked these men and women individually, to invite them to play poker with me or to drive to Greylock. Someday I would like to write an essay on this topic, the economic divide in our society. We may talk all the time about equality in our society, but economically the very rich live in one world and the rest of us in another. The relationships I had with these men and women added immeasurably to my life, I do not mean to be critical of them here. I am merely stating the facts. We liked each other and we worked closely together with each other, but the social lines stopped at the NYU borders. There were a few exceptions, such as Dale and Elizabeth Hemmerdinger and Helen and Martin Kimmel.

Leonard and I did cross the line and became very close with Helen and Martin Kimmel. Helen was a member of the NYU Board of Trustees and a major donor. She and Martin contributed financial support for many projects at the NYU Medical Center and at the square, where they funded the NYU Helen and Martin Kimmel Center for University Life—one of the most beautiful buildings on Washington Square.

The Kimmels introduced me to Bernice Manocherian. Bernice is an attractive, very smart woman who was the first and only woman president of the American Israel Public Affairs Committee (AIPAC) and today continues to be someone who the leadership in the Jewish community calls on for advice and direction. I depend on Bernice and my sister-in-law Helen for helping me through the ravages of old age.

One of the smartest and most interesting people I met at NYU, who became a dear friend was Dr. Ann Marcus. When I was senior vice president, she was a vice president who worked closely with me. Whenever a school at NYU is in trouble, they sent Ann Marcus to fix it. She has been, at different times, dean of the School of Continuing Education and dean of the Steinhardt School of Education. At the present time, Ann is the director of the Steinhardt Institute of Higher Education Policy. We continue our professional relationship and our friendship.

Also at NYU, I worked very closely with the Bronfman Center directors over the years, and they became friends. They each now hold important positions in the Jewish community. They include: Susan Dickman (executive vice president, Jewish Communal Fund), Rabbi Andrew Bachman (executive director, The Jewish Community Project JCP Downtown), Cindy Greenberg (president and CEO, Repair the World), David Rittberg (senior program officer, Charles and Lynn Schusterman Family Foundation), and the current director, Rabbi Yehuda Sarna, who has been directing the Bronfman Center for the last eighteen years. He has given the Bronfman Center an international face. I also worked closely with Dana Raucher, executive director of The Samuel Bronfman Foundation, since that foundation handles Edgar Bronfman's philanthropy.

Furthermore, at NYU, Elisa Guarino, Senior Director, NYU Media Production, has been a close colleague and friend for many years, and her son Logan Richman who designed an early version of the front and back covers of this book.

Jim Gibby, assistant manager of the NYU Reprographics department, published my previous three books: *Politics, Religions and Love*; *For Her Days, Not Her Nights*; and *From Bankruptcy to Billions*. Jim has always helped me both as a colleague and as a friend.

And what would my life have been without Rae Weiss and Bonnie Burns, who were my assistants. I have said over and over again that I could not have achieved what I did in my professional life without Rae and Bonnie. They were the people who typed the letters, answered the phones, made the appointments, and helped coordinate all the work in my office.

Fundraising requires a group effort. Bonnie and Rae were an important part of the fundraising group. I am prepared to say in writing that Bonnie and Rae helped make it possible for me to raise the billions of dollars that I did that helped take New York University from bankruptcy to become a great global academic institution.

Bonnie Burns has been my executive assistant at NYU for more than 30 years and continues to work with me still. She is very smart, has a great sense of humor, and takes her work and her relationship with me very seriously. Bonnie assisted me on every aspect of my work throughout my career at NYU. She has not only worked with me but has become a friend on the deepest level, as she knows every aspect of my life. In addition to her administrative skills, Bonnie has a beautiful voice and before coming to NYU she sang in various places both abroad and in Greenwich Village. So, when I am very depressed with the world, I call on Bonnie and together we sing the songs that were part of my life and her life. Well, she sings, and I hum along, and that always makes me feel better.

And, of course, I spent a great deal of time with the members of the professional staff in the NYU Office of University Development and Alumni Relations who worked at my side for more than 25 years. Today, many of them continue their relationships with me as friends, especially David Koehler, who did a fabulous job as director of the development office for so many years. We could not have raised the billions of dollars that we did without his steady hand. There were also Myra Biblowit, Larry Siegel, Jane Karlin, Laura Fredricks, Marian Stern, Cindy Forbes, and scores of others. Their feelings about me are expressed in the quotes that appear on the back cover of the book on fundraising, *From Bankruptcy to Billions*, that I wrote several years ago. I feel the same way about them.

A special word about Myra Biblowit. After leaving NYU she became the president and CEO of the Breast Cancer Research Foundation. She has done a fabulous job for that foundation and, I believe, Myra is the best fundraiser I have ever met. She and I remain friends.

Myra introduced me to Ann Kern, managing director of Korn Ferry. At one point Ann worked at NYU, but then moved over to Korn Ferry and became one of the most successful people in the executive search world. She and her partner, Jerry Gotkin, live a few blocks away from my apartment in New York and we see each other in a social relationship which I enjoy very much. Jerry has become "one of the girls." We all adore him, and I especially enjoy his visits with me.

Myra also introduced me to Dr. Julie Mitnick, a preeminent doctor in New York City who established Murray Hill Radiology and Mammography. People come from all over the world for Dr. Mitnick's opinion on their breast cancer. he is an icon in that world. It is an honor to know her and to be her friend.

Also, through Helen I met Joan Marans Dim, who worked with Helen as the managing director in the NYU Office of Public Affairs. Joan is a wonderful writer and has written several books including the novel *Recollections of a Rotten Kid*; and three histories: *Miracle on Washington Square: A History of New York University*; *New York's Golden Age of Bridges*; and her most recent book *Lady Liberty: An Illustrated History of America's Most Storied Woman*, which is particularly good.

Due to my interest in Israel and the Middle East, I met Ron Bruder. We worked together and became friends. Ron is the founder and board chair of Education for Employment (EFE), the leading nonprofit job placement network in the Middle East and North Africa. EFE identifies critical skills gaps in local economies, then develops and delivers targeted training programs for youth with limited opportunities and graduates are then linked to jobs with employers, civic and educational organizations.

Ron has become more than just a professional colleague. I do not think I am exaggerating it when I say we have become very, very close friends. He has a lovely estate in Westchester, which I try to visit as often as I can. And when he brings his boat to Florida, he always makes it a point to try to get me "on the boat" and also visits me in my apartment in Florida. We try to see as much of each other as possible in view of the strong friendship we have together.

I want to thank, too, the many other doctors who have kept me alive, including Dr. Larry Chinitz, cardiologist NY; Dr. Paula Rackoff, internist NY; Dr. Stanley Chang, ophthalmologist NY; Dr. Gabriela Goldstein, internist FL; and Dr. Keith Meyer, cardiologist FL; and Dr. Josef Jelinek, my dermatologist, and his wife, Dr. Vera Jelinek.

I must also speak about Dr. Robert Press, whom I met when he was first assigned as the doctor in infectious diseases to care for Leonard, when had come down with an infection in the biliary duct. He worked day and night to find the proper medicine to help Leonard. Eventually he found the right medicine. Subsequently, we became friends and continue that friendship to this day. Dr. Press is now the executive vice president, Medical Affairs, at Maimonides Medical Center.

I must also tell you about Althea Lee who has been my aide and my companion for many years. Althea is a strong, caring woman. I can be a stubborn old lady sometimes. Althea knows how to stand up to me without any complaining. I feel extremely lucky to have found such a marvelous person to watch over me. Althea has endured car trips back and forth between New York City and Palm Beach. She has endured the five-hour trip from Manhattan up to Raquette Lake. Even though living in the woods is not particularly appealing for her, Althea has steadfastly been by my side at Greylock. I would not have been able to finish this book without Althea's encouragement and assistance.

Leonard always complained that I required an entourage around me wherever we went—Fire Island, Westport, Adirondacks, etc.—and he was correct. For reasons that only my analysts could explain, I always needed people around me. Being with Leonard and my family was not enough. Friends were absolutely essential. They added so much to my life, both professionally and personally.

So, as you can see, I have been very lucky with the friends I have had. My jobs at NYU and the American Jewish Congress gave me wonderful opportunities to meet very exciting people who then became involved with me in my work and my personal life. I needed them very much. Friends became almost as important as family—family that was scattered throughout the globe. I never took the time to really thank them. So, before I close this chapter, of my book and of my life let me end by saying to all of my friends and my family—"Thank you very much."

Epilogue

So, my hundred years are over, and they have been phenomenal years for my country, for the world, and for me. We went from the horse and buggy to the automobile and then to the airplane. We made the globe smaller, and I now can travel around the world in less than half a day. Other inventions have been incredible. Electricity made it possible for us to read day and night and to have the telephone, the radio, and television. Medical science has permitted people to live to a hundred and that same science allowed men to leave their footprints on the face of the moon.

Of course, it has not been all good: we saw two terrible world wars and many smaller ones. Those wars destroyed empires, killed millions of people, destroyed old countries and created new ones. Inspired by these wars, terrible weapons were created—the atom and hydrogen bombs—strong enough to destroy the planet.

More recently, we are engaged in a third "world war," with an enemy we cannot see, i.e., the war against coronavirus. In World War I and World War II, the fighting was done by soldiers. In the war against this brutal disease, all of us are involved. As a result, I am a "victim." I am "imprisoned" in my apartment. My building is in quarantine. No one in the building can go out and no visitors can come in. It is like a prison camp. I cannot see my grandchildren or my daughter or my friends. I can contact them only on the telephone.

It is a terrible war, made even more terrible when you cannot see your enemy. It is a strange time for the whole globe. We can only hope that this war, like others, will end and some scientists will come up—not with a new bomb or new bullet—but with a new vaccine. As I write this, a vaccine has been found and it has been reported that Pfizer and Moderna have already produced the needed vaccine which should be ready for use in the months ahead. That will be a miracle. All I wish for at this time is to be free again.

But on an even more personal note, these a hundred years were extraordinary years for me. I went from a one-bedroom apartment with a toilet in the hall to a three-bedroom apartment with three toilets at 29 Washington Square West in the heart of Greenwich Village. I went from a 25-cent lunch at the automat to a $50 lunch at the Gotham Grill and an even more expensive dinner at Daniel or Le Cirque. And I went from a five-cent subway ride from the Bronx to Hunter College on 68th Street to a limousine ride for the same distance that today costs me $100. And I have a weekend house in Westport, Connecticut, and an apartment in Palm Beach, Florida. Who could ask for anything more? Leonard and I earned those changes in our lifestyle through hard work and the great education that New York's educational system gave us.

I had marvelous parents, Malvina and Nathan Bronheim. They nurtured me and gave me every opportunity to get the best education. They encouraged me to go to law school, although very few women were lawyers at that time. And although they needed money desperately, they never suggested I drop out of law school and get a job. The fact that I became a lawyer is largely due to their encouragement and support.

As I mentioned in the book's final chapter, in April 2019, I became a great-grandmother. And like all great-grandmothers, I believe that my great-granddaughter, Elowen, is the most beautiful, smartest, and most adorable baby ever created.

As I look at her, I wonder what will her world be like in 25 years, or 50 years, or in 100 years? Will she spend her summers on Mars and not in the Adirondacks? I only wish I could hold her hand and walk with her through the years ahead. But, of course, I cannot. I can only hope that she will be safe, happy and healthy, surrounded like I was with wonderful family and friends. And I hope that every so often she will think of me and that she will continue the fight for civil rights, human rights, women's rights, and the rule of law—areas that meant so much to me. And if she does, you can be sure I will hear about it wherever I may be.

(Left) As I once was. (Right) As I am now.

A Note on
The Woman in the Room

The Woman in the Room was the beloved, final project of an extraordinary woman, Naomi B. Levine. This version of the manuscript was edited by Sofia Ergas Groopman with the oversight of Ms. Levine's daughter, Joan Kiddon. It was beautifully proofread by Elisabeth Kauffman, and published with the utmost care by Brooke Warner and Lauren Wise at SheWritesPress. The cover, an homage to the movie posters Naomi adored, was wonderfully designed by Julie Metz. We only wish that Naomi could have seen it in its final form.

Notes

Chapter 1

1. Daniel Okrent, *The Guarded Gate: Bigotry, Eugenics, and the Law That Kept Two Generations of Jews, Italians, and Other European Immigrants out of America*, (New York: Scribner, 2019), 69.

2. Joan Marans Dim and Antonio Masi, *Lady Liberty: an Illustrated History of America's Most Storied Woman* (New York: Empire State Editions, 2019), 1.

3. Okrent, *The Guarded Gate*, 69-70.

4. "The Uprisings of The Women." The New York Times, 5 May 1912, https://timesmachine.nytimes.com/timesmachine/1912/05/05/100533174.html?pageNumber=14.

5. It's amazing how many immigrants came here penniless and, through their own hard work and entrepreneurial spirit, were able to accumulate money and buy real estate, big and small. Many became the barons of the real estate world in New York City and throughout the country.

CHAPTER 2

1. Jean Edward Smith, *FDR* (New York: Random House, 2008), 436.
2. Ibid., 458.

CHAPTER 5

1. Jim Callan, *America in the 1960s*, Decades of American History (New York: Facts On File, 2006), 30-31.
2. Ibid., 31.
3. Ibid., 41.
4. G. Calvin Mackenzie and Robert Weisbrot, *The Liberal Hour: Washington and the Politics of Change in the 1960s*, Penguin History of American Life (New York: Penguin Books, 2009), 100.
5. Frye Gaillard, *A Hard Rain America in the 1960s, Our Decade of Hope, Possibility, and Innocence Lost*, (Athens, GA: NewSouth Books, 2018), 263.
6. Callan, *America in the 1960s*, 101.

CHAPTER 6

1. Gerald Ford, "Gerald R. Ford's Remarks Upon Taking the Oath of Office as President," Gerald R. Ford Presidential Library and Museum, https://www.fordlibrarymuseum.gov /library/speeches/740001.asp.
2. NB: Naomi Levine passed away before the current assaults on *Roe v Wade*. There is no question that she would be horrified by the current situation and the leanings of the Supreme Court.
3. Bree Burns, *America in the 1970s*, Decades of American History, (New York: Facts On File, 2006), 44-45.
4. Ibid., 48.
5. As I write this, I have just learned Cindy Greenberg was chosen as the director of Repair the World, a national Jewish co-ed

organization. So, we have at least one Jewish organization that has chosen a woman to be a director.

6. Arthur Hertzberg, *A Jew in America* (New York: HarperOne, 2002), 356-357.
7. Bree Burns, *America in the 1970s*, 76.
8. Ibid., 79.
9. Ibid., 79.
10. Carter, Jimmy. "Energy and the National Goals—A Crisis of Confidence." American Rhetoric, https://www.american-rhetoric.com/speeches/jimmycartercrisisofconfidence.htm.

CHAPTER 7

1. Michele L. Camardella, *America in the 1980s*, Decades of American History (New York: Facts On File, 2006), 69.
2. Ibid., 103-104.
3. Ibid., 33.
4. Ibid., 97.
5. Ibid., 97.
6. Ibid., 97.
7. George Ochoa, *America in the 1990s*, Decades of American History (New York: Facts On File, 2006), 27.

CHAPTER 8

1. George Ochoa, *America in the 1990s*, 39.
2. Ibid., 87.

CHAPTER 9

1. Naomi Levine died right before the birth of her second great-granddaughter, Linnea Naomi Salskov.
2. After the writing of this memoir, Elizabeth became legal counsel at Bob's Red Mill.

About the Author

Naomi B. Levine was a celebrated attorney, activist, and fundraiser. She graduated from Columbia Law School at a time when few women were admitted and went on to pen amicus briefs that were essential to the civil rights cases *Sweatt v. Painter* (1950) and *Brown v. The Board of Education Topeka* (1954). She was the first female director of the American Jewish Congress and played an active role in the Civil Rights movement from that position. She later became an executive vice president of New York University, where she orchestrated the first billion-dollar capital campaign. She passed away in Florida in 2021 at the age of 97. She was a lifelong New Yorker. Four months after Naomi's death, her second grandchild was born Linnea Naomi.

SELECTED TITLES FROM SHE WRITES PRESS

She Writes Press is an independent publishing company founded to serve women writers everywhere. Visit us at www.shewritespress.com.

Irma's Passport: One Woman, Two World Wars, and a Legacy of Courage by Catherine Ehrlich. $16.95, 978-1-64742-305-6. After two European cataclysms disrupt the life of Irma—the wife of the leader of Vienna's Jewish community—she escapes to London and New York, where she restores her life by saving child refugees. This true story, told in Irma's words and narrated by her granddaughter, reveals an inspiring woman who used languages as her passport to a safer, more hopeful world.

Newcomers in an Ancient Land: Adventures, Love, and Seeking Myself in 1960s Israel by Paula Wagner. $16.95, 978-1-63152-529-2. After leaving home at eighteen in search of her Jewish roots in Israel and France, Paula learns far more than two new languages. To navigate her new life, she must also separate from her twin sister and forge her own identity.

Shedding Our Stars: The Story of Hans Calmeyer and How He Saved Thousands of Families Like Mine by Laureen Nussbaum with Karen Kirtley. $16.95, 978-1-63152-636-7. From his post at the headquarters of the German occupation during World War II, Hans Calmeyer surreptitiously saved thousands of Jewish lives in the Netherlands. Here, Laureen Nussbaum describes how Calmeyer declared her mother non-Jewish and deleted her and her family from the deportation lists— and traces the arc of both her life and Calmeyer's in the aftermath of the war.

In the Game: The Highs and Lows of a Trailblazing Trial Lawyer by Peggy Garrity. $16.95, 978-1-63152-105-8. Admitted to the California State Bar in 1975—when less than 3 percent of lawyers were women— Peggy Garrity refuses to choose between family and profession, and succeeds at both beyond anything she could have imagined.

Life's Hourglass: A Memoir of Chasing Success at a Cost by Janice Mock. $16.95, 978-1-63152-005-5. When Janice Mock's stage four cancer diagnosis causes her to examine her career as a successful trial lawyer and the relentless drive for wealth and excess that corporate America promotes, she comes to the realization that she must change in order to make the most of the rest of her life.